CONTENTS

Recipe for Happy Graduates

Ingredients

1 fresh graduate
A small bunch of good friends
1 welcoming family
A handful of enthusiasm
A generous dollop of fun
A pinch of courage

Method

Take the graduate and shake up with
plenty of fun and enthusiasm.

Return to the warm family home
and allow to rest.

Add the bunch of friends, mixing
thoroughly.

Sprinkle in a pinch of courage.

Whip up a crisp CV and spread evenly
over a well-seasoned network.

When the grad is ready and bubbling,
pour out and stir up the jobs market.

Snap up a sizzling hot job offer and
serve with lashings of pride.

Enjoy!

SURVIVE
&THRIVE

A graduate's guide to life after university

SOPHIE & JULIE PHILLIPSON

Book design by Lizzy Tasker
Illustrations by Chris Gilleard

ISBN 978-1-7393347-2-7 (print)
ISBN 978-1-7393347-0-3 (eBook)

First edition 2023

Roots & Wings Ltd.
20-22 Wenlock Road
London N1 7GU

Disclaimer: This book does not provide financial, legal or any other advice. It is for general information purposes only. When making important decisions, you should always carry out your own additional research to suit your particular circumstances, and where necessary, seek independent advice from a qualified professional.

Why you *Need* this book

To recent graduates, this book is for you. Use it to see you through the next exciting (but sometimes daunting) phase from leaving education to the world of work and independence. It's here to help you take control and feel confident and upbeat about your future... survive and thrive with this graduate's guide to life after uni!

It's said that life after graduation is full of opportunity and new beginnings. But, having given your all to the university experience, you now find yourself back home, surrounded by boxes and suitcases, and wondering what on earth to do next. With everything now wide open, a sense of overwhelm can set in.

After the high of graduation, it's not unusual to mourn the end of some 18 years in education, when the only choices you really had to make were what subjects to study and where. This is a time of changes and challenges: relocating, leaving friends, finding paid work, choosing a career, working out how to become financially independent... the list goes on. Uni – whilst arming you with a degree, lifelong friends and several years of incredible memories – doesn't totally prepare you for what comes next.

But it is absolutely manageable, and can even be fun, and we want to show you how. With plenty of stories from graduates who've gone first, we've written a step-by-step guide to negotiating life after uni, packed with practical tips and ideas. From job applications to sorting your finances and looking after your mental health, this book is here to help you devise a plan of action, execute it, and support you along the way.

We hope you enjoy this ultimate guide to life after uni written by graduates, for graduates. If there's one thing we want you to take away, it's the knowledge that you are not alone and, as you will see, there are many different routes to happiness and fulfilment. Whatever you do next, take your time, and don't forget to enjoy the ride.

See what's in store...

Chapters

1. To New Beginnings

We'll cover how to approach your next phase, how it's likely to feel, and talk about the graduation blues, aka the quarter-life crisis. We'll explain how shifting your mindset can drive positive changes.

2. The Best Laid Plans

Practical tips for managing uncertainty, creating a 'big picture', setting goals and making plans to keep you focused and motivated.

3. Take Care of You

A focus on physical and mental wellbeing, spanning fitness, food, stress and sleep, because staying healthy will make this period of change vastly easier to handle.

4. Find Your People

You'll need your social network for relaxation and support, but you've just left many friends behind. We'll help you deal with moving back home and make the most of it, or settle into a new place if you're relocating.

5. What Next? Careers & More...

Your career will be long, so there's no pressure to find the perfect job now. There are plenty of options beyond well-publicised grad schemes you'll need to know about, like entry-level roles with businesses small and large, further education, travel and self-employment. We'll look at the pros and cons of each and point you towards opportunities.

6. Job Hunting: How to Stand Out

With job applications there's only one chance to make a first impression. We'll cover what to prepare before applying – including your CV and online profile – and we'll give you crucial tips for all stages of the process, from cover letters and tests to interviews and assessment centres.

7. The Power of Your Network

We'll bust myths around networking, explain why it needn't be daunting and look at how it plays a lead role in any career. In this chapter, there's also a step-by-step guide to networking, including online via LinkedIn.

8. Why Work Experience Pays

Work experience is what sets grad CVs apart. We'll help you make a plan, find opportunities, apply and get the most out of every placement.

9. Your Money Matters

We're never taught money management, we're all just expected to know it. That's why we've written this chapter, so you can learn how student loans and graduate accounts work, and how to make a budget and live within your means. There are handy tips on saving and a glossary explaining common financial jargon, plus we tell you where to find unbiased resources and financial support.

10. Flying the Nest... Again

Private renting is a bit different from student lets. We'll cover the key differences and help you get clued up so you can avoid falling foul of scams. There's help on finding properties and housemates and we'll look at different types of renting, contracts and costs. You'll also find useful checklists for viewings and moving.

11. Final Thoughts

We look at what 'success' really means and sign off with some motivational words for your new beginning!

1

TO
New
BEGINNINGS

Congratulations! After years of hard work and a lot of fun along the way, you've finally got your degree. Before you do anything else, seize the opportunity for a well-earned break; thinking about your future can wait a little longer. When you feel rejuvenated, pick up this book again, because it's here to help plot your next steps (and it'll still be here when you've had some rest and relaxation!).

Graduation means new beginnings, bringing exciting opportunities, but also uncertainty and challenges to many aspects of your life. So, we'll begin by exploring the ups and downs, with tips on how to approach this next phase, so you feel confident and upbeat about your future.

It's a big change, but it's absolutely manageable.

Until now, life has probably been reasonably predictable. Since early childhood, education has provided a natural progression, but after university, there is no logical next step – choices are wide open; so, unless you're one of the lucky few who graduated with a job lined up, your sense of purpose may seem a little hazy. You might also be adjusting to living back in the family home away from uni friends, juggling job hunting and creating a social life whilst managing on a tight budget.

Adapting to this new life can initially feel uncomfortable and unsettling; but remember that change can be healthy and liberating, and it's essential for personal growth. We'll look at effective strategies for managing these various changes, to help you minimise stress and enjoy life as you move forwards.

How are you feeling?

While some people seem to breeze through the transition from university to 'real life', for most, it's not that straightforward. Expect to experience a rollercoaster of emotions ranging from excitement and joy to blind panic.

Don't worry, this is all quite normal. There are even names for it: "graduation blues" or "quarter life crisis". If you are struggling, know that you're not alone.

Writing down our thoughts and feelings can help us understand them more clearly. **Jot down what's on your mind.**

THE UPS AND DOWNS OF LIFE AFTER UNI

We have spoken to lots of recent graduates and here are some of their typical thoughts and concerns, which may reflect how you're feeling too.

I FEEL...	WHY YOU'RE FEELING THIS WAY	WHAT YOU CAN DO NEXT
Lost, overwhelmed, low	After a lifetime of education revolving around routine, goals and deadlines, the sudden uncertainty and lack of direction can feel daunting, even for the most chilled graduates. If that wasn't bad enough, you've got to start a career in the aftermath of a global pandemic. Now what?!	You can diffuse these feelings of overwhelm by starting to make a plan – setting yourself priorities and small, achievable goals. A little planning can go a long way towards keeping you focused and positive. We'll show you how in 'The Best Laid Plans' .
Clueless about life in general but reluctant to ask for help	Nobody is telling you what to do and, suddenly, you're expected to know about things like tax, tenancy agreements, credit scores, and signing on for benefits as a jobseeker. You don't really know what it is you need to know. But you're embarrassed about asking for help, because you don't want to look stupid. So you feel as if you're on your own.	The 'real world' involves many new life skills. You don't have to know everything, but don't be afraid to ask, you'll learn much faster. We'll take you through some basics and where to find help from reliable sources in our chapters on money and renting.
Under pressure to sort my career	You're feeling under pressure to get a job? Worried about getting the right job? Or have no idea what you want to do? A handful of your fellow grads left university with job offers and work placements. But most people leave uni without a clear idea of career direction. And that's OK.	There are plenty of ways to discover what might suit you e.g. stints of work experience and by networking with people who work in industries that inspire you. See our chapters on networking, careers and work experience for help. Your first job is just a starting point; your career will be long, with plenty of twists and turns. What you try now won't limit you in future.
Frustrated, finding it tough to stay motivated	Job applications are relentless and time consuming. It's tough dealing with rejections, or just not hearing back at all from companies.	Unfortunately job hunting is a long process that requires effort and concentration. (You'll find tips for writing applications in the Job Hunting chapter.) Rejections are inevitable but don't let them define you. It's how you move on that matters. Staying positive is half the battle.

I FEEL...	WHY YOU'RE FEELING THIS WAY	WHAT YOU CAN DO NEXT
Worried that my degree or grades aren't good enough	When pitted against other grads, you think your application won't be taken as seriously because you didn't get the grade you were hoping for, or you didn't attend a top university. Will this negatively impact your chances in the jobs market?	As well as your degree, many employers look at things that give grads the edge, like work experience, interests and volunteering. Focus on those and your course, to show you have skills and personal qualities that are relevant to a particular job. Read our tips in 'Worried About Your University Grades?' (p.88)
Broke, no money!	You've graduated with heaps of debt, there's no more student loan, and it could be a long time before you're earning decent money. Financial independence seems light years away and the cost of living is prohibitive in big cities where work opportunities are more plentiful.	First, it's important to understand that your student loan is not like real debt. What you'll pay back depends on what you earn, not how much you borrowed. And you only start repaying when you can afford to. But there are plenty of sensible things you can do now, like set financial goals, budget, find clever ways to cut costs and look at how to boost your income – all explained in 'Your Money Matters'.
Lonely, I'm missing my uni friends	When you lived together, your university friends felt like family. Now you're living apart, it seems hard to keep in touch, especially when you're all at different stages: some already have jobs, others are travelling. Plus, not everyone speaks openly about how they're feeling. It may also be hard to reconnect with home friends, or to meet new people if you relocate to a new area.	Your social network is crucial for your happiness – for relaxation and support when you need it. You're all going through this together, so do open up to your friends and encourage them to do the same; you can help each other. See our chapter on 'Find Your People'.
Left behind. Everyone seems so far ahead of me	Life suddenly feels very competitive. You're pleased for them, but also jealous of friends getting jobs easily, going travelling and having everything sorted with a clear path ahead.	It's not a competition, even if it feels like that sometimes. Everyone's journey is different and we all work to different timescales. It's important to follow your path. Try not to compare, and remember, people only post the good stuff on social media. You will get there, in your own time.

I FEEL...	WHY YOU'RE FEELING THIS WAY	WHAT YOU CAN DO NEXT
Trapped! After the freedom of uni, I don't want to be living back home	Moving back to the family home feels like a step backwards. You're concerned about the loss of freedom and lack of personal space. But without a job, you can't afford to rent.	Moving back home is the normal route for most graduates, at least for a while. Focus on the positives – not least the chance to save some money – and with some effort and good communication with your family, you can make it work for everyone. Read our suggestions in the 'Moving Back Home' section' (p.64).
Concerned about relocating, but there are limited job opportunities close to home	You have no clue about renting and whether you will be able to afford it. (Student renting was a different ballgame!) How will you find flat-mates and a decent place to live? Moving to a new area could be very lonely.	Relocating for work, while daunting, could be the best thing you ever do. It's a chance to make new friends and get to know an area you've never lived in before. We have loads of tips on hassle-free renting, how to avoid pitfalls, plus a whole section on finding your people.
Torn – I'd really like to travel but feel I ought to find a job	This feels like your last chance to travel for an extended period, before working life puts an end to long holidays. But you're also under pressure to start a career because of your student debt, your parents' views and your friends are starting work. What should you do?	There's no right answer, it's a personal decision that will probably be dictated by whether or not you can afford to fund your trip. But travel is a school in itself, and you're likely to pick up many transferrable skills. One option is to take a 'working gap year', where you travel and work, volunteer etc. (if circumstances allow). We've covered this in more depth in 'What Next? Careers & More' See 'What are my options after uni?' (p.69)
Happy and excited about the future!	Graduation feels like a welcome change from education, and you can't wait to get started in your career. You're really looking forward to the fun stuff, the independence and earning some decent money.	A* for positivity! Start with the Planning chapter to make the most of life ahead.

Develop a *positive* mindset

"You'll never find rainbows if you're looking down."
Charlie Chaplin

How we deal with what life throws at us shapes our very personalities, it is the core of who we are. But positivity is a choice, rather than being innate. It's not a question of pretending a bad situation is a good one, or ignoring what went wrong, it's about looking for the best outcome rather than the worst.

Lots of people struggle with self-belief, particularly at this stage. Next time you think you can't do something, change your internal dialogue. Think about your strengths, what you **can** offer and how you **could** make it happen.

❝ BEING ABLE TO REFRAME YOUR THOUGHTS HELPS YOU SEE POSSIBILITIES - IT'S A BRILLIANT LIFE SKILL TO HAVE. YOU'LL NEED TO WORK ON YOUR MINDSET, SO POSITIVE THINKING BECOMES A HABIT.

OF COURSE, WE'RE ALLOWED TO FEEL SAD OR LOW, WE'RE ONLY HUMAN. BUT IF YOU'RE FEELING NEGATIVE AND YOUR THOUGHTS ARE HINDERING YOUR EXPERIENCE, TRY TO FLIP THE SWITCH, CHANGE THE EMOTION. IT WILL INVOLVE A LITTLE SELF-TALK, TO SILENCE THAT DOUBTING INNER VOICE AND REPLACE IT WITH ENCOURAGEMENT.

LEARNING TO CONTROL AND CHOOSE YOUR MINDSET DOES TAKE TIME AND EFFORT, BUT YOU CAN MAKE IT HAPPEN, AND THE BENEFITS ARE MASSIVE. **❞**

PETER, BUSINESS CONSULTANT

TOOLBOX TO FEEL GOOD AND BE YOUR BEST

Life coaches and youth counsellors recommend the following tools to help you stay positive and embrace the challenges ahead. Check in here anytime you need a gentle reminder, or when the going gets tough.

1. Know you're not alone

The graduation blues are well documented. Everyone handles things differently, but it's important to know that however you're feeling, you're not alone.

2. Talk to people you trust

Your friends are there, even if they're not all close by. You'll need them when you want to relax and have fun, but you'll also need them to blow off steam and support you when you need it most.

Highs and lows during uncertain times are inevitable. Most people will understand how you feel; even if they haven't worked in your industry or graduated from uni, they may still offer valuable advice and could have a refreshing view. So, don't bottle things up. Share your feelings with friends, talk to your family, or a professional counsellor. Don't ever be afraid to ask for help.

4. It's okay not to know

Job hunting, juggling your finances and negotiating the rental market all involve life skills and knowledge that you're unlikely to have been taught at school or college. (We think they should be!)

Doing things we don't feel skilled at can make us uncomfortable. But first, understand that you're not expected to know this stuff – no one does, everyone is self taught. So don't be scared to seek advice from those who've trodden the same path – people are generally happy to help. And remember, life's a journey, you will always be learning.

5. Go easy on yourself

Take time to reflect on what you have achieved and to work out what you want. You're unlikely to know immediately, you'll have to try things out, so just give it a go. Don't feel pressure to find the perfect job; view your first job as exploratory, a career stepping-stone – a chance to scope out an industry and gain some valuable experience, while earning some money.

3. Carve your own path

"Be who you are. Be true to yourself. Do what makes you happy, what you're comfortable with, and if you're doing that, you can't go too far wrong. If you're focusing on pleasing other people, you're not going to find that self-satisfying inner peace. Don't do what you don't want to. Don't be afraid to say no."

Mark, Career Coach

6. Manage other people's expectations

Work out how to respond to the well-meaning enquiries from family and friends. They will keep asking, not just because they're curious, but because they care about you. If you've not had a bite yet, it can sometimes be hard not to get defensive when pressed.

Try explaining, for example, that you're applying for several jobs and waiting for responses, but in the meantime you're volunteering/taking an online course/enjoying reading lots/freelancing/doing some shifts at your local supermarket. Also, take the opportunity to ask if they have any industry contacts who might be able to help you find out more.

> "Different generations have very different ideas on everything. Explaining my tattoos to my parents, that was impossible! Try to explain what you're doing, the reasons why you're doing it and that it's going to make you happy. Show them examples of people or jobs out there.
>
> People can see times are changing, especially the generation coming out of uni now. People are creating jobs for themselves, roles are less defined."
>
> **Hannah, Designer & Business Founder**

7. Appreciate stability

When everything is changing, it helps to have some consistency and stability in your life. Hold on to the things that remain the same whether that's your family, a relationship, good friendships and whatever you enjoy doing.

8. Maintain balance

At university, you might have neglected the things you liked – sports, music, art, reading – because of exams, work pressure, and a frenzied social life. Now's the perfect opportunity to go back to things that once helped you unwind and kept you motivated. So, dust off that trumpet, get back in the swimming pool, and find that sketchbook!

9. Use coping mechanisms

Take comfort from the fact that you have coped with difficult challenges in the past, including major transitions like going to university. What coping mechanisms have worked well for you in the past? These might include exercise, relaxation techniques, hobbies, walking the dog, writing in a journal or even just having a set routine. Find out more about the benefits of routine in 'Make a Plan' (p.32).

10. Focus on the controllables

There will always be things going on in the world that you can't control and that may affect the jobs market, including the impact of coronavirus, Brexit, economic recession, and austerity.

But there's plenty you *can* influence and change. We're going to help you focus on what you can control and make it the best it can be. You've got this!

EVERYONE DEALS WITH CHANGE IN THEIR OWN WAY. ALTHOUGH YOU CAN TAKE ADVICE FROM OTHERS, IT IS IMPORTANT NOT TO COMPARE YOURSELF TO OTHER PEOPLE. YOU MAY DECIDE TO MOVE BACK HOME FOR A WELL-DESERVED BREAK, OR TO TRAVEL THE WORLD, OR TO APPLY FOR AS MANY JOBS AS YOU CAN. TAKING TIME TO REFLECT ON HOW FAR YOU HAVE COME AND TO ACKNOWLEDGE WHERE YOU ARE, WILL HELP YOU DECIDE WHERE YOU WANT TO BE.

ROSS, ENTREPRENEUR

2

THE BEST
LAID
plans

To-Do
- ✓ Job Search
- ✓ Finances
- ✓ Go for a run

Until university ended, you were on a path – to graduation. Your ultimate goal was to get a degree. Now you've got one, you'll need a new plan. With a clear picture of what you want to aim for next, you're far more likely to achieve something you're proud of (and will avoid drifting aimlessly!).

Look at this chapter as an exercise in planning and visualising success. We'll show you how to take control, so you feel confident and motivated about the next phase. We'll look at building your 'big picture': thinking about where you'd like to be with various aspects of your life, identifying any barriers and working out how to get around them. Finally, we'll help you turn this into a workable plan, so you can make progress through small, manageable steps. Let's get started.

We've also included a section on how to adapt to a changed world, and an action list of 20 things to do when you first leave uni.

Take Charge

Professor Sir Cary Cooper, CBE, a world leading expert on wellbeing says: "If you remain passive, thinking, 'I can't do anything about my problem', your stress will get worse. That feeling of loss of control is one of the main causes of stress and lack of wellbeing." *(Source: NHS.uk)*

Taking charge is empowering, but that doesn't mean you need to have your whole life mapped out.

Some people leave university with a clear career plan, but for most, the future is less predictable. And, even if you think you know, you'll inevitably encounter twists and turns, new openings and the odd curveball. This stage is all about development and discovery – finding out who you are, what you love doing, how you'd like to live your life – and it's perfectly OK to change your mind.

> **THERE'S A LEVEL OF PLANNING NEEDED BUT YOU DON'T HAVE TO OVER-PLAN. ALTHOUGH YOU SHOULD CONSIDER YOUR NEXT STEPS AFTER GRADUATING, YOU DO NOT NEED TO PLAN THE NEXT FEW YEARS OF YOUR LIFE. HAVING A GOAL CAN HELP YOU TO WORK OUT WHAT YOU NEED TO DO TO MOVE FORWARD.**
>
> ROSS, ENTREPRENEUR

If you know where you're currently headed and just want to make it happen, skip to 'Make a Plan' (p.32). If you're less sure, read on…

FEELING STUCK?

In our early 20s, when we're just learning about ourselves and what's out there, it can feel impossible to make a decision on what direction we want our life to go. We can feel paralysed, rather than liberated, by the possibilities. The good news is, you don't need to have it all figured out, even the tiniest step is progress. Here are five tips to get you unstuck:

1. Clear your head

Destress and calm your mind so you can start to think clearly. Try some of the simple mindfulness exercises in the 'Take Care of You' chapter (p. 41) or whatever usually works for you: relaxation techniques, sport, talking to a friend, writing down what's bothering you etc.

2. Get to know you

Life decisions start with you. Begin to build self-awareness, think about what truly matters to you, what makes you happy and what would add more meaning to your life.

3. Learn from people who have been there before

Speak to friends and family who graduated before you. What was their post-university experience? You may be surprised to learn just how many of them had (long) periods of unemployment, or started out pursuing what they thought was the career for them, only to end up in a completely different field. And some will have switched careers more than once.

4. Accept that change is part of life

There will be times when you don't know what to do next, or you will make the wrong decision, and that's OK. If things don't work out, you can make a different choice. So just focus on what you might like to try for the next year or so, it's fine to change track later. Gradually, you will discover your purpose and your passions.

5. Take small steps

Set a few attainable goals: just three things to do this month that would make your life better than it is today, for example sort your bedroom, take a daily walk, learn a new skill. These small wins will build your confidence, helping you to embrace change and figure out your next steps.

Breathe. Leaving uni is always going to seem like a stressful time: moving from a structured environment to complete freedom. Suddenly you don't have people telling you what to do; independence is thrust upon you. There's a temptation to review all the options available, but you need to stop and think about what you really want, independent of what parents think or friends are doing.

People feel a huge pressure to know what they want, but you won't know immediately. Take time to reflect; start to build a picture of you: what you enjoy, what interests you, what you want to do in your life, what's important about the career environment and the people you'll be working with.

Chloë, Early Careers Coach

ADAPTING TO A CHANGED WORLD

War, climate change, a global pandemic... With the world in so much turmoil it's easy to feel bleak about our career prospects. But it's important to remember that throughout history, there have been and will continue to be major events and disasters with wide-reaching economic and social fallout – the global financial crisis, recessions, austerity, Brexit. These are things we can't control but that affect our immediate plans and prospects because they impact the economy, the jobs market and graduate recruitment, personal finances, the housing market and our everyday lives.

Worrying about things we cannot change is a waste of energy. Instead, we need to focus on what we can control, where we can make progress now – and that includes our own potential. It is well within your power to build a successful career.

There may be a new 'normal' and perhaps a new status quo, or a change of heart will lead you in a totally different direction, towards a more purposeful role. Or maybe not. But whatever you decide, there's plenty you can achieve related to your career and personal growth.

CAREER WISE, THINK CREATIVELY

Start with you

Begin by reflecting on what feels especially important and urgent. What really matters to you? That might be learning – a new skill or a whole new profession. Or it might be that you want to 'fix' climate change or help people worse off than you. What drives you, what inspires you and what would you like to achieve?

Where are the potential opportunities?

Some sectors are more resilient than others in terms of how well they weather world events. It's wise to keep an ear to the ground and to make sure you're educated and informed about what's affecting the industry on a macro level and, on a micro level, how the businesses you'd like to work for are being impacted. This awareness will help you identify potential opportunities, but you'll also be able to show off your knowledge in job interviews and have more interesting conversations with new contacts you make.

Do you have an in-demand skill you could freelance? Or a smart business idea?

Are you a whizz at Photoshop, know Excel like the back of your hand, or can you whip up a presentation worthy of putting in front of a panel of investors? Leverage any contacts and create profiles on freelancer marketplaces to market your skills and pick up new clients and new projects. And, if you think you have a strong business idea and an entrepreneurial streak, consider writing a simple business plan and having a go. If you choose to return to employment later on, entrepreneurial skills are highly valued by employers.

Do your research and put yourself in the strongest position

Research careers and roles that interest you. Find out what skills or experience are valued, and if you don't already have them (from previous work, degree or outside interests), think how you might acquire them. If traditional work experience is hard to come by, consider volunteering, virtual internships or online tutorials. Read up on industry topics to improve your knowledge.

23

GETTING HIRED:
THE RECRUITMENT PROCESS

Be aware the pandemic has changed the way some businesses recruit people, and possibly the skills and attributes they look for in candidates, too.

You may find the hiring process for some roles is now done completely online, and so you may encounter virtual and video interviews alongside the usual psychometric assessments. And ultimately, if you're hired, you could be working either completely remotely, or alternating between home and a workplace. As someone new to an industry, you may prefer roles that give you more contact time in the office, or you might prefer the flexibility of hybrid working, provided there's plenty of support.

Job search prep

Before you begin your search in earnest, you'll need to prepare a draft CV, get any public-facing social media profiles (including LinkedIn) ready for scrutiny, and then start to build your network.

If you know where you're keen to apply, look into the recruitment process and get in some practice for their psychometric tests. Build confidence for virtual or video interviews by speaking to people via webcam so you can check how you come across. See 'Job Hunting: How to Stand Out' chapter (p.103).

Practise speaking via webcam!

Set yourself a personal challenge

LIFE ADMIN

Take some time to get yourself straight. If you can tend to the areas of your life that can be stressful, such as sorting out your living arrangements, getting your finances in order and finding a healthy work-life balance, you'll be better placed to focus on job applications.

PERSONAL GROWTH

Setting yourself a personal challenge will give you a sense of purpose and achievement, good for building confidence in other aspects of your life and developing emotional resilience. Perhaps try something you might never have done otherwise e.g. take up running with Couch to 5K, learn to play a musical instrument or trace your family tree.

Get your finances in order

EXERCISES IN TAKING CONTROL

If you're feeling unsure of where your life is headed, try some of these useful techniques to help reduce mental clutter and overwhelm, and move things forward.

BUILDING THE BIG PICTURE

Make a mind map

Why?

Mind mapping is a simple way to organise your thoughts, and with it, your life! It'll offer clarity about your goals, what is within your control and what options are available to you.

How?

1. Using a big sheet of paper, start in the middle and work outwards.

2. In the centre, draw or write down how your life looks today. Use pictures or words to represent aspects of your life: career, relationships, fitness & health, money, learning, living arrangements – whatever is most important to you.

3. Next, think about how you'd like these various aspects of your life to develop over the next couple of years. Use keywords or pictures to visualise these thoughts around the edges of your paper.

4. Then, in the space that remains, draw or write what's stopping you from reaching each goal, such as the resources you lack or the obstacles you face. These might be:

a. Personal: unhelpful habits, fears, self-doubt, lack of experience or knowledge

b. Social: people obstructing your progress, or whose help and support you might need

c. Environmental: circumstances or events, either personal or wider world

5. Draw thick coloured paths from your central image to each life goal, crossing the obstacles.

6. Finally, brainstorm everything you can think of to help you hurdle those barriers and reach your goals. While some obstacles (particularly environmental ones) are typically beyond our control, we can think of contingency plans to try and minimise their impact on our progress. Get help from family and friends if needed. Write these along each path.

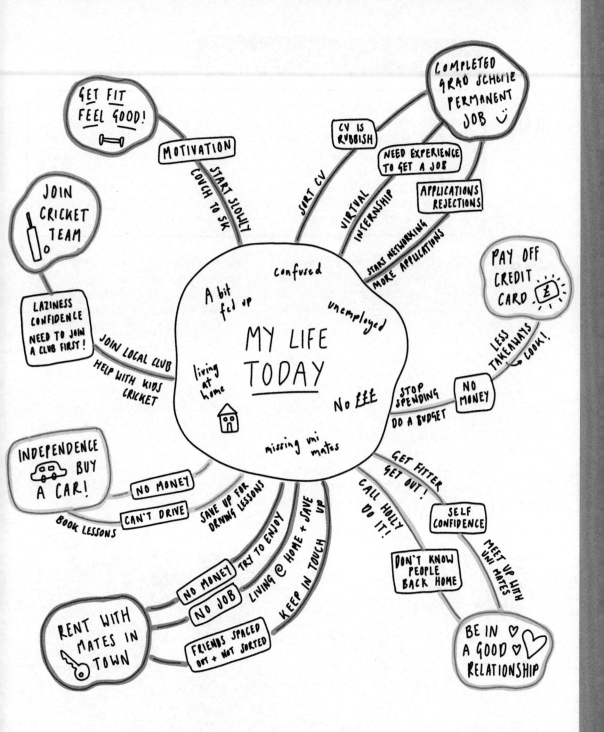

> IF YOU FIND A PATH WITH NO OBSTACLES,
> IT PROBABLY DOESN'T LEAD ANYWHERE.
> FRANK A. CLARK, AMERICAN WRITER & CARTOONIST

Create a vision board

Why? A vision board is a way of presenting your goals and intentions. It's a helpful starting point, even if your goals feel too big right now or too far away. (In the next section, we'll explain how to break them down into manageable steps). If you're a visual learner or like getting creative, you may find a vision board really works for you. It's a very personal thing, fun to do and you can create it however you like – everyone's board will be different. The act of sticking it down makes it feel all the more real and will hopefully provide great motivation every time you see it.

How?

1. Pick up to five things you would like to achieve, in any areas of your life, and give them a timescale – it might be a year, it might be five years.

2. Create your board from whatever you like e.g. corkboard or piece of card. Stick on words or images that represent your goals, using newspaper cuttings, materials, stickers, photos or drawings.

3. Place the board somewhere you will see it most days – in the kitchen, on your wardrobe or above your desk.

4. Once you have completed something, have a fun way of showing you've done it: a big tick across the picture, scribble it out, or if it's a pinboard, move it to a different section.

5. Of course it's OK for your goals to change. If that happens, stick a new goal on top, so it stays relevant and you continue to feel motivated.

Keep a Journal

Why? Journaling helps to clear mental clutter and improve focus. Writing down your thoughts, beliefs and everyday experiences can help you understand them better, acknowledging what's really important, what went well and what didn't, and why you behave and feel as you do. It will help to clarify your values, and form then focus on future goals. Keeping a journal at this time will allow you to reflect on how this exciting new chapter in your life develops. It will also remind you of what's good about your life, your qualities and achievements.

How?

1. Choose whatever format you prefer e.g diary, notes, vlog.

2. Regularly write down three things you're grateful for, three things that made you smile etc.

3. Note anything that is worrying you, why you're stressed about it, what is contributing to the problem and what you could do to help the situation.

Give it a try – you might be pleasantly surprised how easily you come up with solutions.

29

Control the Controllables

This is about letting go of what you can't change and focusing your energy on things you **can** do to start shaping your future.

Try this exercise from Natasha Devon (MBE), writer and mental health campaigner:

If you're feeling overwhelmed or stressed out, it's a good idea to separate out the things that are worrying you, by writing three lists:

List 1	List 2	List 3
Things within your control, that you can sort yourself	Things you can sort with a bit of help from someone else	Things that are completely out of your control

There's no point in worrying about those, it's wasted energy. So screw up list 3 and chuck it away!

Let's concentrate on lists 1 & 2, the things we can control – these will form your basic To-Do list.

Let go of things you can't change, like unemployment figures, or limited graduate opportunities in industries hit worst by the pandemic.

Instead, take control by focusing on small steps to move things forward, like updating your CV, meeting application deadlines or starting a fitness regime.

Make a plan to tackle these goals one at a time.

And reward your accomplishments, however minor – they all represent progress, and will help you stay positive and motivated.

You'll soon feel you're getting your life on track after graduation.

Make a Plan

Time to get organised! You've identified steps to move things along, so you now need to break down your goals into manageable tasks and create a realistic plan to achieve them. Try to build in these three elements: structure, balance and a sense of achievement.

Structure

In uncertain times (and always actually!), it helps to have some sort of framework for your life – to achieve your goals, but also to set aside time for relaxation and enjoyment. Sticking to a routine means we know what we're doing, so we feel more in control and better able to cope with change. It's all about being in our comfort zone. So, stick with your usual rituals as far as you can e.g. wake at 8, check the news, walk the dog...

Balance

Good physical health will boost mental wellbeing, by increasing energy levels, lifting your mood and helping you stay calm. So be sure to look after yourself, with a balanced diet, regular exercise, plenty of sleep, socialising and fun. (See 'Take Care of You', p. 41). Doing more of the things we enjoy or find inspiring is great for our general wellbeing!

A sense of achievement

Setting yourself a personal challenge can provide a sense of purpose and fulfilment that will give you motivation and confidence in other aspects of your life. Constructive activities or acquiring skills also help validate you, to yourself and other people, showing that you're using your time in a positive way. So, sign up for a sporting challenge, join a volunteer programme, rediscover drawing, experiment with cookery, learn to code, whatever suits your interests.

Find a personal challenge!

Job hunting? Stick to your plan

Job hunting can be extremely time-consuming. But a clear action plan will keep you focused, because you know what you'll be doing during the day and you can line up something to look forward to once it's done.

Even if you're feeling down because you're getting rejections, resist the temptation to let your routine go. Honour the good parts as well as the work: the enjoyable elements will boost your mood, a just reward for the hard graft of job applications.

If you're not yet clear on career direction, there's still plenty of groundwork you can do: plan small tasks like perfecting your LinkedIn profile, preparing a CV, desk research or an informal fact-finding chat with a family friend.

MONTHLY PLANNER

MONDAY	TUESDAY	WEDNESDAY	TH

PLAN WELL *Work smarter*

Whether you're WFH or job hunting, follow these pointers to maximise productivity. Treat your search like a job itself.

1. Review your priorities and set a few realistic objectives for the day.

TIP
Use a planner.
Alongside to-do lists, a calendar or planner can help you stay organised, setting daily goals and keeping track of application deadlines, interviews etc.

2. Tackle difficult tasks when you're most productive.

Are you a morning person or a night owl? Your motivation naturally ebbs and flows throughout the day, so do the tough stuff like applications during your peak productivity periods.

3. Introduce variety.

If tasks are becoming repetitive or boring, mix them up.

4. Take plenty of breaks.

Include exercise and fresh air to increase energy levels, clear your head and keep you motivated.

TIP
Try the Pomodoro technique, a time management method which breaks your working day into 25-minute chunks, each followed by a five-minute break (and a longer break after four bursts of focused work). Over time, it can improve your attention span and concentration.

Or check out some of the many available time management and goal tracking apps to help keep you fired up and on schedule.

5. Separate work from home life.

Create a workspace away from distractions, try to stick to set hours, and then properly switch off at the end of the day: shut down your laptop and 'go home' – relax, rest and recharge.

TOP *20* THINGS TO DO WHEN YOU LEAVE UNI

Get cracking with this to-do list (who doesn't love crossing things off?!). Add your own items or use these small but important goals to get off to a good start and lift your mood.

Relax & reflect

1. Take a break!

☐ When you first leave uni, start by taking some well-deserved time for yourself: duvet days to binge watch TV, getting outside for fresh air and nature, or sleeping as much as you want. Whatever it is, indulge yourself, unwind and chill.

2. Reflect

☐ Revel in what you have just achieved at university – brilliant! Think how far you have come.

Getting Settled

3. Unpack and declutter

☐ Sort out your uni stuff and declutter your space of anything and everything revision-related, it can feel very satisfying!

> **TIP**
> Don't throw away big projects or important pieces of work as they may well come in handy later. Pass on revision notes and books to students who could use them and recycle any papers you won't need again.

4. Create your space

☐ Wherever you're living for now, create a comfortable space to suit your needs. If you're job hunting or WFH, make a workplace separate from your relaxation area. You'll be far more productive than if you work from bed or slump on the sofa. Try to find somewhere with good natural light, away from distractions.

5. Catch up with friends and family

☐ Revision and exam season can turn us into hermits, where socialising goes out of the window. And moving away from uni friends can leave us feeling quite isolated. So, plan social time with friends and family, which will lift your spirits and help you feel connected. Life is more than just finding a job, so make the most of the spare time whilst you have it and enjoy yourself!

looking after yourself

6. Start an exercise routine

☐ Apart from the obvious physical benefits, exercise is a great stress reliever and mood booster. So get active with a fitness regime, regular bike rides or just a daily walk.

7. Get back on track with your interests

They might have taken a back seat during exam season, but now's the time to go back to the hobbies and sports you enjoy and help you unwind. Join a book club, rediscover the joy of singing, or dig out your camera and unearth your flair for photography – whatever floats your boat. If you have moved back home or to a new area, it's a great way to meet like-minded people and make new friends.

Dig out your camera!

8. Read (or listen) for pleasure

After weeks of revision, curl up with a good book, get lost in another world and just enjoy reading for pleasure. Research shows that reading can increase empathy and improve our relationships with others as well as boosting our general wellbeing. If reading isn't your thing, try listening to an audiobook or get stuck into a great podcast.

Money matters

9. Get a temporary job to bring in some cash

If money is tight, arrange some temporary work that you can fit around job hunting e.g. freelancing, tutoring, dog walking, bar work. Ask relatives if they want any odd jobs done, like car washing or DIY. Or reap the benefits of your decluttering efforts and sell unwanted stuff on eBay or Gumtree.

10. Open a graduate account

If your student account doesn't automatically transfer to a graduate account, consider switching, to benefit from preferential terms such as an interest-free overdraft to help you pay off debts and take control of your finances.

11. Set up a budget

Track your money coming in and money going out, so you can live within your means and avoid running up debt. It's a good idea to set small achievable goals e.g. pay off £300 of my overdraft in the next three months. See more finance tips in 'Your Money Matters', p. 171.

Personal fulfilment

12. Set yourself a challenge

A personal challenge that stretches you will help you thrive and prove you made good use of your time: become a decent cook, ditch one bad habit, climb a mountain, walk 10,000 steps a day, or whatever rocks your socks!

13. Volunteer

There's a huge need for volunteers now, whether it's supporting the NHS, charity fundraising or local community projects. And it's win-win: you'll make a positive difference to people in need, it's personally rewarding and you'll gain valuable transferable skills that look great on any CV.

Search GOV.UK for volunteering opportunities in your area or contact local charities and community groups directly.

14. Upskill. Keep learning

Boost your employability by enrolling on a short online course, watch tutorials to hone a useful skill, read around an industry topic to expand your knowledge, or take up a new language.

Groundwork for career

15. Write a basic CV

Once you have a solid template CV, you can easily adapt it for each job application to highlight your most relevant skills and attributes.

16. Set up or spruce up your LinkedIn profile

Make sure your professional profile is visible on any platform that's important for your chosen industry.

17. Sort your social media footprint

Use tight privacy settings so you don't put off prospective employers!

18. Get networking

Arrange your first networking conversation, online or offline.

Life admin

19. Register on the electoral roll

This is the official list of names and addresses of everyone registered to vote in public elections or referendums. It's also used in crime prevention, calling people to jury service and for checking credit applications.

It's important to be on the list so you can vote, but also to start building your credit rating in case you want to borrow money in the future (a mortgage/loan/credit etc.) It's simple to sign up: search 'Register to Vote' on GOV.UK.

20. Get organised

Start making a plan of the things you need to do over the coming months relating to your job search, finances, living arrangements and more. Set yourself small achievable goals and plan leisure and social activities to keep you motivated.

TO DO LIST

HOW TO SET GOALS *(& Stick to Them!)*

Taking a step back and looking at what we want to achieve can be very therapeutic. We set goals to get motivated, become more productive, notice an improvement, re-invigorate ourselves and earn some self-appointed brownie points!

Here are simple tips for setting goals with sticking power:

1. A few at a time

Having too many is a non-starter. Focus on a few so you feel the benefit of actually achieving.

2. Simple steps

Break down individual goals into small, achievable tasks – if you keep it simple, you'll grow accustomed to the change you're aiming for, and will keep going.

3. Mini Milestones

Set dates to give yourself a time limit. Quantifiable measures can help you monitor your progress e.g. I will apply for three jobs this week. Mini milestones give a good reason to celebrate or reassess (don't give up!)

4. Celebrate the little wins

If you're on track to achieve your goal, reward yourself when you finish; but make sure you also celebrate progress along the way, and your commitment too.

5. Mix it up

At this stage of life, many objectives will revolve around finding a job, earning or saving money, living arrangements etc. But set some goals around things you LIKE doing e.g. walk the Pennine way, round up your uni friends, sing in a rock choir... whatever matters to you.

6. Write it down

Dr Gail Matthews, Psychology Professor, studied people from different walks of life, including entrepreneurs, educators, health workers, artists, lawyers and bankers. She split the group into those who wrote down their goals and those who didn't. She discovered the likelihood of achieving goals increases by 42% if you simply write them down every day.

7. Visualise

Visualising goals can help you achieve them (it may sound strange, but athletes do it all the time!). It really is a case of seeing is believing. Whatever you aspire to do – work in finance, quit smoking, run a marathon – rather than dwelling on reasons why not, visualise what success looks like and how it feels, and picture the processes you'll need to go through. Visualisation actually trains your brain and promotes positive thinking, which will help keep you on track.

8. Tell people

Talking about what you want to achieve makes it real and holds you accountable. Tell your nearest and dearest so they can encourage you! Some goals (e.g. improving fitness) have dedicated apps to help you, cajole you and share your progress with friends, so find one you like.

Good luck!

Summing Up

The transition from student life to the working world can be challenging, and everyone adapts differently, but these tips and tools should help you make a strong start. Learning how to manage change is a key life skill, which will help you maintain a happy, balanced lifestyle and avoid the graduation blues.

"You get one crack at life. Try to fill every single moment with things you love doing and try to eliminate all the things you hate doing. You may or may not be successful in traditional terms, or career terms, or financial terms, but by God you'll be happy."

— Bruce, leisure company CEO

3

TAKE
CARE
OF
you

Your top priority right now – and it really is more important than anything else – should be your wellbeing. And looking after our physical health can protect our mental health.

In this chapter, our aim is to help you design a routine that accommodates staying active, eating nutritious food, keeping hydrated, spending time outside in the fresh air and getting enough immune-boosting sleep.

Sticking to a healthy routine requires a little willpower and discipline. But don't worry, everything we recommend isn't only good for you, it should also be enjoyable and either relaxing or invigorating (promise!).

And remember, by looking after your physical health, you will be able to transition between university and real life all the more easily, and even enjoy the journey. Use our worksheet at the end of this chapter to map out your own wellness goals and form healthy new habits.

Movement

Apart from the obvious physical benefits, exercise is a great stress reliever and mood booster – and it need have nothing to do with expensive gym memberships. Hopping on a bicycle for a leisurely ride, taking a long brisk walk, playing touch rugby with some friends in the park, and yoga classes on YouTube are all completely free.

So, find something you enjoy and blend it into your weekly routine (something you may be yearning for now school's out!). It's wise to alternate vigorous exercise, like high intensity interval training or running, with gentler, low-impact exercise like walking – as well as taking rest days – so you don't overdo it. If in doubt, listen to your body.

If you've never done much exercise before, try the free Couch to 5K app which you can download to your smartphone, and follow the sessions like a podcast. And if that doesn't sound appealing, just get outside and head to the greenest spot you can find for a walk. If you're spending long periods sitting at a desk writing job applications, the fresh air will refresh you and lift your spirits – as well as get your body moving.

Football Fridays!

Fuel

Good eating habits and wholesome nutritious food can keep your blood sugar levels steady, help you stay alert and full of energy, and keep mood swings at bay, so you feel good and better able to cope with stress.

That means eating regularly (don't skip meals), staying hydrated and choosing foods that release energy slowly into the bloodstream. Include wholegrains, fruit and vegetables, bread, pasta, lentils and beans in your diet (switch these up each day) as well as protein-rich foods like lean meat, fish and nuts that help your body function and stimulate your mind too.

But, whilst you need to ensure your diet is nourishing to your overall health, treating yourself occasionally or even every single day is absolutely OK and will help you to maintain a healthy, positive relationship with food.

Just aim to get the nutrients you need in as natural a form as you can, from whole foods rather than ready meals or fast foods. But, as life can get busy, these quick options can always be enjoyed in moderation.

Some experts urge people to try and eat at least five portions of fruits and vegetables per day while others recommend eating 30 portions of different plant foods – including beans, pulses, nuts, seeds and herbs – each week to maximise the range of nutrients, vitamins and minerals you get. This is a fun challenge to try, because it's harder than it sounds!

There are lots of confusing and conflicting messages about what is right and wrong, so we recommend keeping it simple: eat a balanced diet, stay fit and treat yourself in moderation.

And remember, hydration is essential to health, and critical to brain function. Even mild dehydration can slow down body functions, leaving you feeling sluggish, moody and unable to think clearly. It can also affect concentration, give you short-term memory problems and cause anxiety. Aim to drink at least two litres per day, and more if you're doing exercise.

And, look, we don't want to be bores, but now's the time to curtail habits and vices that can cause long-term harm. Opt for healthful behaviours such as exercise which can give you the biggest rush of all!

* Keep it simple!

Meatless meatballs

Green & Lean Smoothie!

The BEST savoury muffins

Food Inspo

Breakfast of champs

Speedy Pesto & prawns

Destress

Whilst we can't totally prevent stress, we can learn to spot the signs and manage it effectively.

> ❝ **Don't feel bad for feeling bad around mental health and depression. You're allowed to feel a certain way, you shouldn't feel guilty about it. If you feel like crap, you feel like crap and you don't need to be apologetic about it.** ❞
>
> Rikesh, Ambassador for mental health charity CALM

A small amount of stress isn't bad; it keeps us focused, alert and helps us perform under pressure. But stress overload can be dangerous, and affect mental and physical health. When it comes to how much stress we can tolerate, we're all different: some people thrive on challenges that make others crumble. The important thing is to know your own limits, recognise the signs early on and take steps to reduce stress.

Mental health charity Mind says that, when we're stressed, we might feel irritable, aggressive, impatient, over-burdened, anxious, nervous or afraid. Our thoughts might race and we may not be able to switch them off. We might feel unable to enjoy ourselves, uninterested in life, or a sense of dread, loneliness or neglect.

When we suffer from stress, we might find it hard to concentrate, or make decisions. We might eat too much or too little, smoke or drink more than usual, or be restless or tearful.

People who experience severe stress can sometimes have suicidal feelings. If you're concerned that stress is affecting your health in any way, it's time to seek help from a professional. Start by speaking to your GP.

And remember you have managed stress in the past: exams, the grind of revision, social situations, family problems, difficult relationships. Coping mechanisms are different for everyone. Think about what has helped you in the past, and turn to those same strategies again. Just like exercise, build those things into your daily routine.

"HAVING YOUR OUTLETS - WHETHER IT'S SPORT, SINGING, COOKING OR DRAWING - IS SO IMPORTANT. KNOW THEY'RE YOUR THINGS AND GIVE YOURSELF THE TIME TO DO THEM."

– MATT, FOUNDER OF FC NOT ALONE
(THE WORLD'S FIRST MENTAL HEALTH FOOTBALL CLUB)
& AMBASSADOR FOR CALM

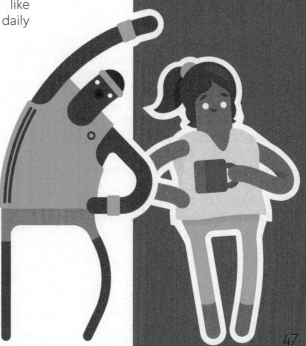

Build coping strategies into your daily routine

Mindfulness

Mindfulness is an increasingly popular way of reducing stress, improving general wellbeing and helping you sleep better. It is a mind-body approach, which focuses attention on the present moment, using meditation techniques.

It can positively change the way you think, equipping you to manage challenging situations rather than feeling overwhelmed by them. One of the simplest ways to start practising mindfulness is to work on your breathing.

Yoga teacher Hannah Aylett, recommends these simple exercises to reduce stress and find calm.

Meditation Exercises

Find a seated position

Close your eyes

Place your hands on your knees

Breathe in and lift your shoulders up to your ears

Exhale, relaxing your shoulders down

Repeat three times

Roll your shoulders, forwards then backwards

Gently twist your torso from side to side to release tension

1 Place one hand just below the ribs

2 Place the other hand on your belly

3 Inhale and exhale slowly through the nose, making the exhale longer than the inhale.
This will help relax you.

4 Focus on expanding the belly and the lower ribcage to take the breathing away from the top of your chest

Repeat 10 times

Controlled breathing is easy and calming:

❝ It's meditation for people who can't meditate. ❞

Dr Belisa Vranich, Psychologist and author of Breathe

YouTube, podcasts and apps have lots of videos/audios to try – find a style that suits you. (Many apps offer a free trial period). Our top app picks:

Headspace

Described as a "gym membership for the mind," it teaches mindfulness and meditation techniques in as little as 10 minutes a day

Calm

Meditation and sleep stories

Buddhify

Mindfulness and easy-to-follow guided meditations for calm and sleep

Deep Breaths!

Talk

They say it's good to talk. Problem is, for too many of us, "talking" is an intermittent flurry of messages on WhatsApp. Nothing beats a deep and meaningful conversation with a really close friend, so pick up the phone or go and see them. It's crucial to make time for this in your week.

Talking something through will help you make sense of how you're feeling. It may help you realise that looming sense of dread can be replaced by excitement, or it might help you build an awareness of what you need to do next.

And if you can't talk, then write. Many people find that jotting down their thoughts and feelings in a notebook helps them sleep better and reduces stress. Regularly committing the chaos of the mind to paper is a really good way to make sense of things and process your thoughts.

Most of us have those days when we feel a bit low or a little anxious, but if it's becoming a regular occurrence, it's a really good idea to seek help from outside your friends and family. There's more on how to find professional help on p.53.

> " When I'm really stressed the important thing for me is to speak to people — my coach, or others around me, not bottle it up. Especially speak to your best friends, they know you better than anybody, so listen to their advice in those situations, and reach out for support. "
>
> Chloë, Careers & Life Coach

Sleep

Sleep boosts the immune system and helps the body to repair itself, so it's really important not to starve ourselves of shut-eye. We all need different amounts but, for most adults, it's somewhere between seven and nine hours a night.

If you're struggling to nod off, stay away from stimulants like caffeine and alcohol in the hours before lights out, and swap stressful TV shows for a bath and a book. Switch off electronic devices for a few hours before bed as their blue light suppresses melatonin, making it harder to fall and stay asleep.

Pay attention to the temperature in your bedroom. In order for you to fall asleep, it needs to be on the cooler side, but not cold. If your room is too bright, test a black out blind. You can buy cheaper, stick on versions if you're not quite sure you want to invest in one yet.

When you don't get the rest you need...

Here's how to power through on very little sleep

Cast your mind back to when you had to get up for a really early flight or train journey, or you danced the night away until 5am and still made it to your 9am lecture. It's amazing what the body can do on the odd occasion you get very little sleep.

If you're facing an important event like exams or a job interview after a restless night, don't panic, these things might help...

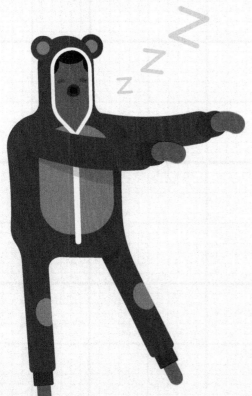

1 It might briefly feel like torture, but taking a cold shower is the best way to wake up your body and your mind. If you're nowhere near a shower, splash your face with cold water or rub two drops of peppermint oil between your palms and breathe in.

2 Eat food high in fibre and protein to fuel your day and keep you fuller for longer.

3 Have a coffee, but don't overdo it, especially if you're not used to it (you could get the jitters and end up feeling worse). Caffeine is a well-known stimulant, designed to keep you alert.

4 Take a power nap. Some experts recommend drinking an espresso before napping for no longer than 25 minutes. This is just enough time to make you feel rested without feeling sluggish – and you'll wake up just as the caffeine kicks in.

5 Go for a walk and stretch your body. It's amazing how a little movement can re-energise you, especially if you do it outside in the fresh air.

Resources

Professional Help
If you're concerned about your mental health, help is out there. Start by visiting your GP's surgery and talk to your doctor about how you're feeling. They should be able to refer you for treatment or recommend a course of action.

Youth Access
Youth Access offers information, advice and counselling services for under 26s, often free of charge. **youthaccess.org.uk**

CALM
(Campaign Against Living Miserably)
CALM is a charity that supports people going through a whole host of mental health issues including anxiety, addiction, depression, eating disorders, financial stress and suicidal feelings. CALM's phone lines are open from 5pm until midnight, every day of the year on **0800 58 58 58** (nationwide) or **0808 802 58 58** (London). **thecalmzone.net**

Mind
Mental health charity Mind has lots of information and resources on its website. Its Infoline – an information and signposting service that you can ask about mental health problems, treatment options and where to get help – is open Monday til Friday, 9am til 6pm on **0300 123 3393** or text **86463**. **mind.org.uk**

NHS
The NHS has a really useful webpage on insomnia, with causes, solutions, and a sleep self-assessment tool that will help you gauge whether or not you need to see your doctor. **nhs.uk/conditions/insomnia**

" It's tough taking that first step to see a counsellor, but it's great once you've done it; just having that first conversation is amazing. I've done it, I'd recommend it. Making that first move is important, but you're thinking here's this human I've never met and I'm sharing some of my deepest stuff with them. So I think chatlines can be very helpful. I can see why it's difficult conversing with someone so far removed, but you're not going to see them, they are there to help, you'll feel so much better, and it will have no negative implications on your life, only positive. "

Matt, Founder of FC
Not Alone

HEALTHY HABITS
WEEKLY WORKSHEET

Fill me in to hold yourself accountable.

One thing I'm grateful for:

This week I want to feel:

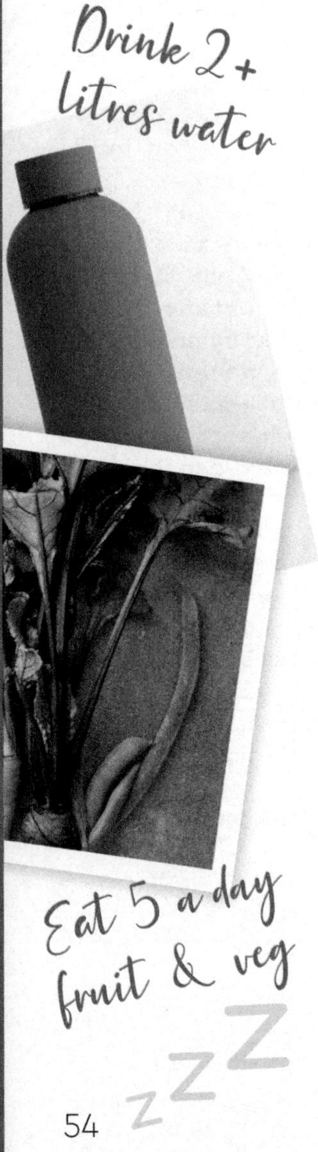

Drink 2 + litres water

My healthy habits	Mon	Tues

Eat 5 a day fruit & veg

z z Z

Get my body moving!

One thing I want to do before the week is through:

_____

Meet a good friend

Wed	Thurs	Fri	Sat	Sun

"A friend may be waiting behind a stranger's face."

Maya Angelou,
Author, Poet & Activist
(from Letter to My Daughter)

4

FIND
YOUR
People

This chapter is all about avoiding the graduation blues by having that all-important social network of friends and family for relaxation and support when you need it. We look at how to find your people (whether you're relocating to a new place or returning to your hometown) and if you are moving back in with the folks, how to make that work, for everyone.

Your Social Network

Leaving your close circle of friends and your buzzing uni social life can be tough and, initially, the months after graduation can feel quite lonely. That's not surprising once you understand loneliness is often triggered by life transitions (e.g. graduation, bereavement, relocating, becoming a parent etc.) You don't have to be alone to feel lonely; it's a feeling of being 'disconnected' from the people around you. But the good news is, that even when we feel isolated, we can nurture and build social connections by reaching out to family, catching up with old friends, and making new ones.

Your social network is important

Keep up with friends

Reconnect with family

Find new people (hometown or relocating)

> 66 WE ARE HAPPY WHEN WE HAVE FAMILY, WE ARE HAPPY WHEN WE HAVE FRIENDS AND ALMOST ALL THE OTHER THINGS WE THINK MAKE US HAPPY ARE ACTUALLY JUST WAYS OF GETTING MORE FAMILY AND FRIENDS. 99 DANIEL GILBERT, HARVARD PSYCHOLOGIST, PROFESSOR, AUTHOR & HAPPINESS EXPERT

Value uni friendships

Once you go your separate ways, it's easy to let uni friendships fizzle out. But you're all going through the same thing and more than anyone else, it's these friends who best understand the mix of emotions you're feeling. That's why it's really important to open up, talk and support each other. Set up a regular catch up, make sure it actually happens and share the highs and lows!

Try not to compare

New graduates often worry about being left behind when friends find jobs, move into a city house share, or go travelling and generally seem to have their lives mapped out. But it's not a competition and you will get there; it's crucial to do what's right for you and at your own pace.

" Post uni, talking to my friends about their job applications, interviews, internships, grad schemes, flat shares, travelling (any plan really), would fill me with dread and, if I'm honest, sometimes jealousy. I couldn't help but feel like everyone else really had their sh*t together. Well, with hindsight and a few more years behind me, I can confirm this absolutely was NOT the case! Of course, a few friends absolutely nail it, but the others don't talk about having zero social life, the crappy interviews or the 30 applications they did before getting a reply... yep, most people will be feeling exactly the same as you! "

Lotty, Senior Creative Production Manager

"I think students' main worries when they leave university relate to moving out, money, and getting a successful job in comparison to their peers. People immediately feel they're on the back foot when they leave university, and everyone else seems to have it figured out. The main thing they worry about is that they are behind other people. But everyone gets there in their own way. Everyone has unique experiences, there are no set tracks, it's about random opportunities that come up, so just be open to that."

Chloë, Early Careers Coach

Kalkidan started Sancho's, an ethical clothing and lifestyle business straight after graduation:

" It was hard at first, when friends took a more 'normal' route – you compare yourself to others. I kept wondering if I had made the right decision. I was really nervous about it.

But once we focused on the opportunities, we realised that although there are costs now, they will pay back in the long run, so why not give it a go. Once we accepted that, we stopped comparing ourselves to others. Life spans are wide, people have so many different experiences, challenges, accomplishments. "

Be sensible with social media - live *your* life

During your final year, you probably barely had the time, let alone the inclination to scroll through countless profiles and stories but once you're less busy, social media can become a huge distraction. Everyone else seems to be having a far better time, but don't be fooled...

"The reason we struggle with insecurity is because we compare our behind-the-scenes with everyone else's highlight reel."

Steve Furtick, American Pastor, Songwriter & Author

Research shows that young adults with high social media use seem to feel more isolated than those with low social media usage. One study suggests that limiting social media to 30 minutes a day may lead to a significant improvement in wellbeing. So, minimise scrolling and give your social feeds a makeover: unfriend and unfollow negative people and replace with motivational, uplifting accounts.

Use social networking for the invaluable tool it can be: to facilitate – but not replace – human interaction. It's ideal for identifying groups of like-minded people, or keeping in frequent touch with friends, but it's no substitute for socialising face to face.

Make an effort to see people

If you're not yet working, it can be tempting to shut yourself away, particularly if you're feeling a bit low and under pressure to find a job. Understandably, you might choose to shy away from those friends who seem to have it all together and keep talking about their fab new job (while you're firmly unemployed) or their gorgeous new boyfriend (when you're hopelessly single). They don't mean to make you feel bad, but they do. It's perfectly fine to see those people less, but don't shut out the world. Instead, surround yourself with positive people who perk you up and make you feel good. After all, we're social creatures and it's crucial for our mental health to interact with people on a regular basis, and face to face, not just through our phones. Besides, enjoying time with friends is a great stress reliever. Meet up to talk through troubles, have a rant and a laugh, commiserate or celebrate. It's always going to lift you, no matter what stage you're at in life!

Making *New* Friends

Whether you're finding your feet in a new place, or settling back in your hometown, there are plenty of ways to meet new people and make lasting friendships. Bear in mind that social satisfaction is not dependent on knowing loads of people, it's the quality of relationships that really matters. We just need a handful of close friends and family members to properly engage with, enjoy their company, confide in, give and receive support.

1. Be proactive, make a plan

Be reassured that you can soon start to feel less lonely by taking small steps. Simple social interactions can give you positive feelings that build over time. For example join a dog walking group or app; you'll find people often stop to chat when you're out with a dog, plus it's a perfect way to exercise, destress and make some yappy dogs happy too! Whatever your talents or interests, there will be something you can try.

2. Choose enjoyable, meaningful activities

Rekindle old hobbies, take up a new challenge, join local classes, clubs or teams. You'll already have something in common with the people there, so it's a natural way to strike up a conversation and make friends.

3. Friends are made not found

Be prepared to put in time and effort: research suggests it takes 50 hours of socialising to make a casual friend and 200 hours to build a really close friendship.

4. Try volunteering

Volunteering not only benefits a good cause, while giving us a sense of purpose and making us feel good, it's also a wonderful way to collaborate with people who share our values and passion. Google local volunteering opportunities and share a few hours of your time each month.

5. Community spirit

If you want to feel properly connected to your neighbours, get involved in local online groups or community centre projects, where you can really engage with people, build relationships and get to know the area.

6. Reach out to old friends

Moved back home? You might be living far away from uni friends, but the chances are several of your schoolmates are in a similar position. Message them and suggest a catch up. It might end up as a one-off beer but, equally, it could open up a whole new social circle.

7. Eat together

In most cultures, people have eaten together for generations. So much more than sharing food, it's for celebrating, bonding and communicating, and a symbol of shared life. So, abandon your ready-meal for one and rustle up a simple supper for housemates or colleagues (or your family). Keep costs down by inviting everyone to bring a dish, or if cooking doesn't ruffle your truffles, suggest a takeaway night and split the bill. It doesn't matter how you do it, the company is more important than the cuisine!

8. Say 'yes!'

"Find a way to say yes to things. Say yes to invitations to a new country, say yes to meet new friends, say yes to learn something new. Yes is how you get your first job, and your next job, and your spouse, and even your kids."

Eric Schmidt, Former Google Executive Chairman

9. Expect the best, not the worst

Don't assume everyone is too busy for conversation or just won't be interested in you. Be open and friendly, people will warm to you. Just start with a smile and a simple hello.

10. Be aware of others

When you first move to a new area or job, it can take a good while to really settle in, so don't worry if you don't feel great. Everyone feels lost or lonely at times, even those who seem to have it all together and know absolutely everyone. Tell someone how you're feeling, even if it's difficult to express. Most people will want to help, just as you would if the shoe was on the other foot. And if others are in a vulnerable position (e.g. starting work), be aware of what they might be going through and chat to them.

"IF YOU'RE MOVING TO A NEW LOCATION, DO YOUR GROUNDWORK BEFOREHAND. DEVELOP A LOCAL NETWORK; SOCIAL MEDIA GROUPS ARE GREAT FOR THAT. JUST TALK TO PEOPLE, IT'S AS SIMPLE AS THAT. FIND GROUPS THAT SHARE YOUR INTERESTS OR HOBBIES, CONTACT FRIENDS OF FRIENDS, OR REACH OUT TO PEOPLE IN YOUR WORKSPACE; EMPLOYERS OFTEN ORGANISE SOCIAL ACTIVITIES TO PROMOTE A GOOD TEAM ENVIRONMENT. OR ASK COLLEAGUES ABOUT THE AREA. IDENTIFY GOOD PLACES TO SEE AND EXPLORE WHAT'S AROUND.

IF YOU'RE MOVING ABROAD, YOU'LL USUALLY FIND THAT NATIONALITIES LIKE TO CONGREGATE TOGETHER, SO YOU CAN ALWAYS FIND GROUPS AND PEOPLE TO HELP YOU; AND THAT APPRECIATE THE CHALLENGES OF RELOCATING TO A NEW COUNTRY OR UNDERSTANDING A NEW LANGUAGE.

SOMETIMES YOU JUST NEED TO IMMERSE YOURSELF. IT'S SCARY, BUT ONCE YOU'RE THERE YOU'LL QUICKLY FORGET HOW SCARY IT INITIALLY SEEMED!"

MARK, CAREER COACH

Need help?

If feeling isolated is causing you stress or affecting your health, seek professional advice from your doctor, or contact mental health charities such as Mind, CALM (Campaign Against Living Miserably), or online support community Elefriends. For more information about these resources, see Take Care of You' (p. 53).

Moving **Back** Home

How to make it work...

For most graduates, moving back home with family will be the most likely option, at least for the short-term while you get sorted with work. After several years of fun, freedom and personal space, the prospect of living back home can feel daunting. There are of course plenty of advantages, but the situation needs to be managed sensitively, so it works for everyone.

Here are some simple tips to ease the transition:

Think of the benefits
Don't view it as a step backwards, but as progress towards a big leap forward to financial independence and adulthood.
Take the opportunity to learn to manage your own finances. Living on lower rent (or rent-free) will allow you to save and buy your own things. You can be totally focused on job hunting and starting your career, surrounded by supportive family and home comforts, which might be a welcome relief from student housing! You can hone your cooking skills and help with maintenance around the house, all of which will come in handy when you're in your own place. It's also a chance to eradicate memories of you as a stroppy teenager and build more adult bonds with your parents. So, try to be diplomatic (and tidy!) and just make the most of the situation while it lasts.

Reshape your space
Clear out the remnants of your teenage years and your uni clutter. Redecorate, accessorise and make your space reflect the present-day you.

Communicate early on
Have a conversation to understand what's important to both you and your parents and establish new boundaries e.g. whether you'll contribute financially, where you could help around the house, and how they feel about the comings and goings of friends or partners.

Have a plan
Even if it's not set in stone, having a target date for moving out will be helpful for your parents and can ease that feeling of being stuck.

"It will be good to have the security of family around, when everything else in your life involves such huge change."

Charlie, final year geography student

Have a plan!

"I'LL LIVE AT HOME AT LEAST UNTIL I GET A JOB, AND PROBABLY FOR THE FIRST FEW YEARS WHEN I'M WORKING. IT'S THE BEST CHANCE TO SAVE A BIT OF MONEY TO INVEST IN SOMEWHERE LONG-TERM."

KIRAN, MATHS POSTGRADUATE STUDENT

"After working and renting in London for a couple of years, I moved back home to pursue a different career path.

Living at home in your 20s is becoming a reality for more and more of our generation, but it can be hugely positive! I found it unexpectedly liberating. It has allowed me to focus on myself and my career, slow down and take control.

With massively reduced living costs, I'm able to save money and have started clearing the debt I racked up in my early 20s. Now I can dip in and out of my social life in London.

It also helps to create an adult relationship with your parents, so they do understand that things have moved on since you were 18!

So I'd say, if you're moving back home after uni, embrace it and make the most of the situation. Use it as an opportunity to take a breather and focus on what you want and how you will make it happen. You're not going to be there forever, so enjoy it."

Lotty, Senior Creative Production Manager

TAKE THE TIME TO BUILD
AND MAINTAIN MEANINGFUL
CONNECTIONS WITH PEOPLE
YOU CARE ABOUT.

STRONG RELATIONSHIPS
ARE KEY - PERHAPS
THE KEY - TO A HAPPY,
HEALTHY LIFE.

5

WHAT NEXT

Careers & more

work & play

We've split this chapter into three parts, because it's packed full of stories, insights, information and guidance that you'll need to know about to kickstart your career. If you're orderly by nature you can read it from start to finish. And if you've got a short attention span, we've got you: dip in and out whenever you need help with something specific.

PART 1: WHAT ARE MY OPTIONS AFTER UNI? (pp. 69–89)

Your career options explained, from employment to entrepreneurship, and from micro-businesses to blue chip firms. We'll also talk you through further study, career gap years, and what to do if you didn't get a 2:1.

PART 2: HOW TO CHOOSE THE RIGHT CAREER AND COMPANY (pp. 90–97)

We look at why workplace culture is so important. And, take our quiz to help you contemplate your career direction.

PART 3: THE JOB SEARCH: WHERE TO FIND OPPORTUNITIES (pp. 98–102)

We cover eight different ways to find job opportunities and throw in some helpful tips.

WHAT ARE MY OPTIONS AFTER UNI?

So, what's next after uni? If you made the most of campus careers services and recruitment fairs while you were a student, it might have seemed like grad training schemes were the only way forward, but actually, there are so many more options.

This section is designed to give you food for thought, by exploring all the different routes into work, as well as options like self-employment, further study and travel. We'll weigh up the differences between working for large and small companies and we'll hear from three grads who opted for entrepreneurship and started their own businesses soon after leaving university.

Whatever you decide to do, remember this is only a start. Whatever job you secure fresh out of uni is by no means a life-long commitment. So, for the next couple of years, just find something that feels right, give it a go and see where it leads you.

"When you're young you're a blank canvas, you have the power to add any colour, dimensions, objects you desire; you're in charge, you can make those decisions."

Jill, Sales & Marketing Director

YOUR OPTIONS AT A GLANCE

GRADUATE TRAINING SCHEMES

Students generally have a high awareness of graduate schemes offered by large employers by the time they leave uni (they tend to be well advertised on campus).

These structured programmes combine working and training, with some leading to professional qualifications. They are common routes into the public sector, the Armed Forces and large corporates, especially in sectors like accounting and consultancy, banking and finance, engineering, law, technology, and retail.

Schemes usually last between one and three years and provide a broad introduction to a particular industry. You'll typically get to work in different teams and departments, which will help you work out what you really want to do, while building your skills and industry knowledge.

Quality training, high earnings potential and attractive starting salaries mean competition is fierce for the top schemes. Some of the Times Top 100 graduate employers receive 650+ applications per vacancy for their structured graduate schemes. The application process can be lengthy and time-consuming, so it's wise to apply early, because some organisations don't wait around to fill places and will close once they are full.

Don't give up if you missed out first time round: you are eligible to apply for most programmes up to three years after graduating. So, consider getting relevant experience elsewhere and reapplying later. And, of course, there are other routes into these organisations. You may be able to apply for an entry-level graduate job, try a speculative approach or look for internships.

"I started on the Tesco graduate scheme where I did buying (pet food) and also product development (home baking), which was a fantastic experience. Once I was on the scheme, I realised food product development was the career for me. Before I joined, I hadn't known much about the role, or realised it could be an option. Broader training schemes give you a little taster. As long as you understand what you want and are able to talk to the right people, you can generally move around different departments within your company."

Rebecca, Food Product Developer

ENTRY-LEVEL GRADUATE JOBS

The vast majority of graduates apply directly for entry-level positions, normally advertised on jobs websites and LinkedIn. These tend to suit grads who have an inkling of the sector they'd like to work in, or the company they'd like to work for. Even if the starting salary is lower than a grad scheme, you can progress faster by gaining on-the-job experience in one specialism or department.

Entry-level graduate jobs are still very competitive, but the application process might be slightly less demanding and onerous than for graduate programmes. You may also find more openings, and in a wider variety of businesses, large and small, across all industries. Numerous companies hire graduate talent without creating specific or structured training programmes.

WORK FOR AN SME

What is an SME?

A small or medium-sized enterprise (also called an SMB) is a business with fewer than 250 employees. A micro business has fewer than 10 employees.

A third (34%) of graduates will be employed by a company with fewer than 250 employees and one in six end up working for a small business with fewer than 50 employees, according to Destinations of Leavers from Higher Education. SMEs make up over 99% of the business landscape here in the UK, so it's highly likely that you'll end up working for one at some stage in your career.

Don't miss out by focusing your job hunting efforts squarely on big corporates known to hire graduates. Smaller companies and the UK's thriving startup scene can offer exciting careers with tons of responsibility, and real opportunities to make an impact and feel valued.

Small companies don't usually take part in campus recruitment drives or offer structured graduate programmes, nor do they typically have close relationships with universities. They tend to rely more on social hiring, speculative approaches, recommendations and referrals to find new talent. The result is a 'hidden' jobs market ready to be tapped by you! You might have to dig deeper to find those opportunities, but there are plenty of rewarding roles to be discovered.

Unlike the strict application procedure for graduate schemes, openings in SMEs can pop up any time of the year: they hire whenever they need people, and many will consider candidates that speculatively approach them, even if no vacancy has been advertised.

So, be proactive, hunt down and target SMEs in industries that interest you. Use your network to see if anyone has connections at those companies, search for real and potential opportunities, and then make contact, by phone, email and/or LinkedIn. They will probably be delighted to hear from you! Just think, less than 10 years on from graduation, you could be sitting on the board of the next Airbnb, Instagram, or Deliveroo. They all started small too...

"AT UNIVERSITY, YOU HAVE ACCESS TO LOADS OF THE TOP GRAD SCHEMES, BUT THERE'S NO FORUM FOR SMALL COMPANIES. UNI CAREER FAIRS ALL HAVE THE BIG CORPORATE FIRMS FROM THE TIMES TOP 100 GRADUATE EMPLOYERS LIST, BUT YOU NEVER REALLY HEAR ABOUT SMALLER COMPANIES OR STARTUPS WHERE I THINK YOU EASE IN QUICKER AND YOU FEEL LIKE YOU'RE WANTED MORE."

CHLOE, POSTGRADUATE MARKETING STUDENT

BIG OR SMALL COMPANY: WHICH WOULD SUIT ME BEST?

Would you flourish in a small dynamic company or could you fly higher in an established blue-chip? Both have plenty to offer, but it's important to understand the differences and how they relate to your personality, preferences, motivations and what you are looking to get out of the early stages of your career.

Learning & Training

Large companies have greater resources and may contribute more to your training, whether that be through a structured graduate scheme or outside professional development, by sending you on courses and training sessions to learn new skills. In addition, from the day you join, you will be surrounded by a broad range of co-workers with a wide variety of skillsets, putting you in a great position to learn fast from people who are experts in their field.

SME recruits might not have a formal training programme or defined managerial support. Often you learn on the job from more senior colleagues, supplemented by online and offline training courses. This hands-on style of learning suits plenty of people. But, in some companies, there may be very little support at all. After a brief introduction, you'll simply be expected to work things out as you go along.

"Big companies can be a useful training ground, even if you want to work for a smaller company eventually. You have exposure to more experts early in your career so you might learn more, quicker."

Jill, Sales & Marketing Director

Career Development

Large firms will typically offer the opportunity to develop your career in multiple locations and divisions, possibly overseas, with continued training and learning from experts within the business. But, in smaller organisations, there may be less scope for internal career moves, relocating, or changing career direction, meaning future opportunities lie outside the company.

But there are career benefits to SMEs: many tend to be less bureaucratic, offering a more flexible, autonomous environment, with an openness to new ways of working, and the freedom for employees to carve out their path to suit their strengths.

And, while a big name on your CV undoubtedly looks great, don't underestimate the value to employers of small business experience. It suggests you are a motivated self-starter, with an abundance of transferable skills and ideas, alongside any technical knowledge and specific expertise you will have gained.

73

Pay & Benefits

Always look at pay and benefits – which might include private healthcare, dental care, gym memberships or a company car – together as a package and consider what is of most value to you personally. Pensions are an investment in your future, so a generous employer pension contribution is valuable to just about everyone. But you may feel as though private healthcare – given that we have the NHS – isn't as useful to you as a starting salary that would allow you to move out of your family home.

A small company is unlikely to match the competitive packages that may be offered by large corporates, however this could be outweighed by the chance to collect new skills, gain responsibility quickly, and climb up the career ladder faster.

"In a large company, particularly a benevolent one, everything is there for you: if you have a grievance, there's a process; if you want to change career, there's a process; you can see a clear career path, everything is done for you. I think, when you're in your 20s, a large organisation is a good place to learn the ropes, find out what you enjoy, what type of work you like, what styles of management suit you or don't. And it's all good training if you ever have your own business subsequently. But, you do have to play by their rules. Some people are very happy to live in that paternal, protective, nurturing and structured environment, while some are less suited."

Monica, Business Adviser

Some company benefits include gym memberships or a company car!

Personality

An ideal candidate for SMEs is a self-starter. You'll have the chance to shine, but it will be very much down to you. You will need to be a flexible 'all-rounder' who is proactive and willing to get stuck in, be curious and ask questions. You will most likely be an independent thinker, possibly with an entrepreneurial spirit and unafraid of risk or uncertainty.

On the other hand, if you thrive on structure and organisation, and like the idea of a specific job scope and clearly defined career progression, then you may settle more quickly in a larger, established corporate.

"In large companies, sometimes you need to fit in to stand out, so it's important to understand what you're going into. Look at the message a company is communicating on their website and social media – the culture, company values, how it brands itself, and how they speak to potential customers and engage with their staff. In the corporate world it's about understanding the rules and adapting to fit in. It's either for you or it isn't and don't be afraid to recognise when it isn't."

Mark, Career Coach

Culture

Working for a company with a great culture will make a huge difference to job satisfaction. Companies of all sizes know it's possible to be professional while still having fun: plenty organise social activities like ping pong tournaments, bake offs, fitness classes, cooking workshops, wine tasting evenings, and inspirational speakers. Some even welcome dogs to the office. Some firms do more socialising with colleagues than others, so if having friends at work is important to you, this should be a consideration when deciding where you might want to work.

But culture isn't about office perks. It's the 'personality' of the organisation which affects everything from how comfortable you feel putting forward ideas in meetings, to how you're recognised for great work, to how valued and engaged you feel.

If some big corporates seem faceless and intimidating, you might feel more engaged in a smaller, friendlier environment. Cultural fit is all-important for small workforces, so you're likely to find yourself part of a close-knit team of like-minded people with shared values working for an SME.

But in companies of all sizes, there are some that do culture brilliantly, and some that don't. You should spend time seeking out companies that treat it as a business priority. (Businesses that really care about their culture will usually mention it in their job ad and certainly on their website.)

Multiple surveys suggest it's actually the largest companies that have the lowest levels of employee engagement, while businesses with fewer than 25 employees have the highest.

"Small business owners know their greatest asset is their staff and they are far more likely to treat them as individuals and recognise their needs. By having a committed and loyal workforce that has a say in how the organisation is run, the smallest business has a bigger advantage."

John Wright, Federation of Small Businesses (FSB)

Job Security

Job security is often a consideration for those weighing up whether or not to work for an SME. In reality, plenty have been operational and thriving for decades. The bigger risk is with brand new companies in their infancy, including well-funded startups that can disappear almost overnight. However, large companies are not immune to job losses either, especially in tough economic times.

For those grads who don't plan to stay in their first job for years and years, and who don't have dependents to worry about, job security will be less important than gaining industry experience.

You'll probably find that different sizes and types of business appeal at different stages of your life and it's easy to change from one to the other to find what suits you best.

INTERNSHIPS & WORK EXPERIENCE

If you are struggling to get a full-time job, or you're unclear about your career direction, try to get work experience in industries that interest you. Whether that's a hands-on placement or a virtual internship that you do from home, it's an excellent starting point that'll help you find out what you want to do without committing.

An internship might even lead to a permanent role but at the very least it should improve your employability, expand your network and perhaps earn you a bit of cash. The majority of internships must now be paid at least the minimum wage and many leading employers now offer paid work experience. (There's more on this in our Work Experience chapter, p.159).

"EXPLORING DIFFERENT JOBS WAS REALLY HELPFUL FOR WORKING OUT WHAT I WANTED TO DO. I WORKED PART TIME IN RECRUITMENT AND GOT SOME EXPERIENCE BUT SOON REALISED IT WASN'T FOR ME. IT'S TRIAL AND ERROR. LEARNING ABOUT SOMETHING AND ACTUALLY DOING IT ARE TWO COMPLETELY DIFFERENT THINGS."

ELLY, RECENT GRADUATE

SELF-EMPLOYMENT & BUSINESS OWNERSHIP

ENTREPRENEUR, FREELANCER, CONTRACTOR, CONSULTANT, RETAILER, FRANCHISEE, SOLE TRADER, GIG ECONOMY WORKER:
there are loads of ways to earn money without being an employee. Many grads supplement their income after graduation by freelancing in all sorts of areas, as copywriters, web or graphic designers, administrators, social media managers, and many more.

Some take this further and end up working for themselves longer term, finding their skills or qualifications are in high demand. Others find that a compelling idea and an entrepreneurial spirit draws them towards starting a business.

In this tough jobs market, an increasing number of grads may be tempted to do their own thing, but it's important to go into it with your eyes wide open. Weigh up the pros and cons before you dive in, to be sure that the self-employed or entrepreneurial life is right for you.

Chloë launched a successful career as a self-employed life coach:

"The only thing I needed to finance was the coaching course, other than that it was just buying people coffee. That's the beauty of what I've been doing, it's essentially creating something out of nothing."

Freelancers & Contractors

Freelancing or contracting is well-suited to those with a profession, trade or craft who don't plan to hire employees and build a brand. You are self-employed and hired by different companies to work on various projects. And, in some sectors, such as IT or television production, hiring contractors for short projects is really common. Sometimes it proves a useful route into permanent employment.

It can take a while to build your reputation but don't feel you have to start off working for free or at a significantly reduced rate. You are still performing a task and adding value and should be compensated fairly. Your client base will grow with time but, in the meantime, there are plenty of online platforms that match talented freelancers with people and businesses that need work doing.

> "Try to think rationally about your approach. Be well organised, very money savvy, and be open to opportunities, because you never know when something is going to come about. Be prepared to network, speak to people, try to build connections. You're going to have to sell yourself, but that's what will keep you front of mind when opportunities arise. Just be a nice person, if you're able to get along and connect with people, that's going to do you wonders going forward. You really have to do that when you're freelancing, it's imperative."
>
> **Rikesh (RKZ), Menswear Writer, Photographer & Musician**

Entrepreneurship

Do you have an idea for a business? Are you prepared to take on the financial risks in the hope of rewards in the future? Are you able to fund your living costs as well as your entrepreneurial exploits? Success is largely dependent on having the necessary skills, real passion and unrelenting perseverance. Entrepreneurship can be an extremely rewarding life, but it's high risk and it doesn't suit everyone.

> WHEN IT COMES TO ENTREPRENEURSHIP, HAVING A BIG IDEA IS LESS IMPORTANT THAN BEING THE RIGHT TYPE OF PERSON. IT'S A CHALLENGING PATH, PAVED WITH EXCITEMENT AND UNCERTAINTY. YOUR BUSINESS CAN TAKE OVER YOUR LIFE AND IT REQUIRES THE RIGHT SKILLS AND MINDSET TO BE A SUCCESSFUL ENTREPRENEUR.
>
> LIZZIE, FOUNDED A BUSINESS SUPPORTING STUDENTS STUDYING AND WORKING ABROAD

If you're serious about starting your own business, research the various incubator and accelerator programmes offered by organisations – including some high street banks – to help fledgling startups or small businesses grow. They tend to offer services free of charge for an initial period, including mentoring, training, office space, resources, networking, and access to finance.

Setting up a limited company is very different from being self-employed. Depending on how your business is structured, you'll be taxed differently, and you may be responsible for employees, too. You'll need to get clued up on these responsibilities and we suggest seeking professional advice on financial, legal and HR matters.

Is the self-employed life right for me?

Self-employment does offer many attractions; the freedom to make your own decisions for one. Then there's flexibility to work when and how you want, and a sense of pride over everything you create or achieve. This all contributes to high levels of job satisfaction, and considerable earnings potential if you are successful.

Being your own boss might sound like the dream, but not everyone can handle the pressure of being ultimately responsible for everything, from providing the goods or services, to growing your business through marketing and sales, to managing your people, finances and tax affairs, to chasing down late payments. While you're behind every success, you also have to face every failure.

Especially in the early days, it can feel lonely and you can struggle to stay motivated and focused, so it's wise to have a supportive network of mentors and advisers whom you can consult and learn from.

One of the biggest challenges is building your customer base. You'll need the confidence to put yourself out there, expand your network and look for potential opportunities everywhere. You'll have to be prepared to deal with risk and uncertainty, including an unpredictable income, plus the fact that work can take over your life at times. Taking time off for more than a day or two can seem like an impossibility.

> **What's the difference between freelancing and permanent employment? Stress levels!** You need to have a lot of self belief and conviction that everything is going to be OK. About 90% of the time, you're probably freaking out, figuring out when your next job will come. I think I started freelancing too early on in my career. A lot of my mentors are freelance, but they have built their skillset and reputation to such a point that they don't need to look for work. When I started, I was relatively unknown, so had to produce really high-quality work, but also actively pursue opportunities.

Rikesh (RKZ), Menswear Writer, Photographer & Musician

The self-employed life inevitably requires hard work, tenacity and perseverance, but it can be super rewarding. You get to pursue your passion, make your own choices, learn loads and enjoy a varied work-life. Don't let the fear of failure put you off: it's not easy, it might not make you rich, but there's a strong chance you will feel happy and fulfilled. And whatever the outcome, know that companies really value enterprising, entrepreneurial individuals, should you decide to go into employment later.

> I thought I could always go back into industry if my business doesn't take off. Nowadays, employers look favourably on entrepreneurship and people trying out things. They call it 'intrepreneurship': having resourceful employees that can solve your business challenges.

Michael, Innovation Consultant

If you want to go ahead, be sure to get to grips with how it all works. Talk to as many people as you can who've followed the path of self-employment, particularly within your industry. Read articles and watch videos. Learn from the mistakes of others who've gone before you! Visit the 'Working For Yourself' section on GOV.UK to find out if your enterprise should be set up as a self-employed sole trader, a business partnership or a limited company and check out the relevant legal obligations and tax information. As well as GOV.UK, look for help on starting your own business at MoneyHelper and HMRC (the government department that handles tax).

If you're self-employed, you are responsible for your own tax affairs. You will need to register with HMRC and complete an annual tax return, whether you are making a profit or loss. It's a really good idea to find an accountancy firm that specialises in working with the self-employed, so they can help you with your tax return and answer your questions.

ENTREPRENEUR CASE STUDY:

KALKIDAN LEGESSE

Founder of Sancho's Ethical Clothing & Lifestyle Shop in Exeter

Kalkidan and her partner Vidmantas started their ethical clothing and lifestyle shop with just £1,500. Here's her story:

I studied PPE at Exeter University, which included a year working for NGOs in Greece and Ethiopia. I've always felt my life had to play some role in sustainable development. My journey as an entrepreneur started when my aunt back in Ethiopia sadly lost her husband and daily life became difficult. She's a fantastic crafter, so we devised a plan where she would weave beautiful scarves for me to sell here in Britain. This almost quadrupled her income and helped see her two youngest kids through school. That's how we started.

Ethiopia suffers from low trade and bad perception. My goal was to bring unique, high quality clothing and lifestyle products back to the UK to sell so we could send back hard currency. Vidmantas and I decided to build our business ethically, with strict buying criteria. We pay all our craftspeople a fair wage, and we're committed to transparency in the production model so our customers can trust that all items we sell are ethically made. This reflects the kind of future, security and environmental policies we want to see. And people want to buy from socially responsible companies, it makes them feel they can make a difference.

Just after I graduated, I noticed the local council in Exeter was offering free pop-up spaces for independent retailers. We applied and were given a store that was a good size but had not been well cared for, so it needed preparation, which Vidmantas did while I booked a

SANCHO'S

ETHICAL CLOTHING & LIFESTYLE

very long, cheap flight to Ethiopia to buy stock. With the money we had left after buying a return ticket, I bought as many beautiful scarves, baskets and boxes as I could from local markets.

Three weeks later we opened, and ran our pop-up shop for three months, holding parties, inviting friends, meeting people, getting to know what it means to work for yourself. Looking back now, I think all graduates initially have a sense of confusion, while they're figuring out what they need to do. For us those few months gave us a chance to see what life would be like as retailers and business owners. It was wonderful. It helped us feel rooted and connected, and we made just enough money to do a bit more of it.

We also entered the National Santander Entrepreneurship Awards – one of the UK's largest student and graduate business competitions – and were named runners up. That earned us a small cash prize, mentoring and startup support, as well as self belief that we had a good business idea.

For me, the best bit of entrepreneurship is the freedom and the opportunities for creative expression. The worst is the hard work: 12 hour days are normal for us. I also underestimated the time it would take to grow a strong brand (years).

It was tough when our friends took a more 'normal' career path. I did worry if I had made the right decision. But that's the value of a partnership: when I was feeling nervous, Vidmantas would encourage me to look at opportunities. Eventually I stopped comparing myself to others.

It really doesn't take anything spectacular or special to start a business, you've just got to trust yourself, start doing it and learn the necessary skills as you go.

ENTREPRENEUR CASE STUDY:
CHLOE GARLAND

Founder of Quarter-Life, a coaching business for 20-somethings

Chloë started her own coaching business to help graduates and young adults work out what they really want to do and how to get there. Read her story:

Like so many other people, I was really terrified about what I was going to do after graduation. I was not excited about the future. To me it was just really daunting. So I decided to speak to a life coach, and it turned out to be one of the most valuable experiences I've ever had. It helped me figure out what fundamentally motivated me, making decisions so much easier.

Coaching is a technique developed in the 70s and 80s to help people accelerate their personal development, from where you are now to where you want to go. Unlike therapy or counselling, it's non-advisory. The coach's job is to ask questions, reflect back what their client is thinking, pick up themes and ideas that you had perhaps not realised about yourself.

It fascinated me so much that I decided to train to become a coach. I had also noticed the lack of support that exists at the end of education and I decided to focus on this age group as I couldn't find anything similar out there. Creating something of my own seemed interesting, exciting, something I would be proud to talk about, so I thought I'd give it a go. Now I'm working with other organisations as well as private clients.

The beauty of it was that I had very low start-up costs. I already had a laptop, and I turned my attic into an office, so all I needed was to pay for a course that would let me become a qualified coach.

The worst part of running a business on your own is the loneliness, which sets in after the novelty wears off. To combat this I built a network of people who have been very generous with their time, resources and skills, people I can call on every month and who've introduced me to others. Listen to other people, that's the way to learn, and say yes to everything, because you never know what opportunities are out there.

Of course it helps that I love what I do. Seeing the people I coach – who are feeling stuck, unsure or overwhelmed – figure out what they're passionate about, what they're motivated by, and that little light come on, can turn any rubbish day into a really great one.

MICHAEL BEAN
Innovation Consultant

Michael started his career on a grad scheme in insurance, before going back to uni to do a Master's in Business Administration (MBA). After launching a tech startup, he now works in innovation. This is his story:

After university, I applied for all sorts of jobs because I didn't know what I wanted to do (studying geography left that decision wide open!). I ended up working in client management for an insurance company. Five years on, I went back to school to do an MBA at Cambridge University. I am a big believer in continuous learning and had aspirations to be a leader, and to find out more about the inner workings of business.

It was a very expensive one-year course, but I felt it was worth the investment, as I thought it would increase my earnings potential. It was there I caught the entrepreneurial bug. I spent evenings attending talks by successful founders and venture capitalists, and participated in hackathons. It was cemented during a project with a fellow student, where we worked up an idea for an insurance technology startup, which could solve an existing problem in the industry we had both worked in. When our proposal won a university competition, that was validation that we were onto something.

After our studies finished, we decided to co-found the startup. At first, we both lived off our savings while we collected evidence to prove our idea could work. We planned to approach venture capital firms later and ask for funding so we could build the technology. I worked on the technical aspects and business development, tapping up old industry contacts. My co-founder came from a legal, operations and finance background so she tackled those areas.

Our idea proved tricky to get off the ground. We needed to sign up lots of big corporations to make the business work and we underestimated how long it takes to make a sale. After nine months, we were only halfway towards our goal. It was an emotional rollercoaster. You live and die with every conversation. We'd have a positive discussion with a would-be client and think 'we're going to be millionaires', and then we'd never hear from them again. That could be demoralising, but it meant the wins were sweeter. Having a co-founder really helped – to mentally pick me up and to bounce ideas off. We set targets to keep us focused. I don't think I could have done it alone.

In the end, we decided it wasn't viable, but the experience was incredible, and I wouldn't have got my current job without it. I'm now an innovation consultant in the insurance industry – a role I love. Basically, I help big insurance companies spot opportunities to develop, grow or do things better.

My advice is don't do entrepreneurship for the sake of it. Whatever idea you work on must be solving a real problem. Make sure you validate that problem before you spend too much time and money on it, and really get to know your customers.

Entrepreneurship: What does it take?

"I think it's important to get experience in your sector first, whether you're freelancing, working for a company, or setting up something on the side. You're never going to know everything, but really understanding the sector you go into is very important. And you'll also learn basic things about the working world, about structure and how to execute plans."

Alessa, Founder and CEO at
Top Tier Impact

"MAKE SURE YOU UNDERSTAND YOUR NUMBERS – CASHFLOW IS KING! SO MANY PEOPLE GO OUT OF BUSINESS BECAUSE THEY'VE NOT INVOICED PEOPLE, AND THEY'VE NOT CHASED TO GET THE MONEY IN. THAT'S ABSOLUTELY CRUCIAL. THINK ABOUT HOW YOU'RE GOING TO FINANCE YOURSELF FOR THE VARIOUS STAGES ALONG THE WAY."

CLAIRE, BUSINESS COACH

"Starting a business when you're young can be lower risk; you have less to lose than when you have responsibilities like a house and family. It might not work out, but it can bring you closer to a bigger, better opportunity. Passion and ambition are key. Aim high! Always keep learning – none of us are the perfect finished package. Building a business is a constant evolution. That's what keeps it interesting and fun."

Ben, Co-Founder of an HR software company

"It takes some gumption. It's a far riskier move than working for a big corporate. You have to be hardworking and motivated. You need creativity to come up with the ideas and you need to be open, humble and flexible, because you can't always stick with your ideas."

Michael, Innovation Consultant

"WHEN MANAGING FREELANCE AND PORTFOLIO CAREERS, WORK OUT WHERE YOUR INCOME (OR REVENUE) WILL COME FROM. THAT IS YOUR PRIMARY CONCERN, WHILE YOU DEVELOP IN OTHER AREAS. MANAGE YOUR TIME WELL. THE BEAUTY OF A PORTFOLIO CAREER IS PEOPLE TEND TO ENJOY WHAT THEY ARE DOING. IF IT'S A NEW IDEA, UNDERSTAND WHETHER THERE'S A MARKET AND WHO YOUR COMPETITORS ARE AND WHAT THEY'RE DOING. YOU'VE GOT TO DEVELOP A CUSTOMER BASE AND PUT YOURSELF OUT THERE: USE SPACES LIKE FREELANCER SITES AND SOCIAL, OR NETWORKING GROUPS. UNDERSTAND WHAT YOU'RE GETTING INTO, THEN GIVE IT EVERYTHING YOU'VE GOT, AND LOVE IT."

MARK, CAREER COACH

"People think being an entre-preneur is living the dream, but the reality is it's such a slog. You won't ever feel qualified, a lot of it is wing-ing it, but if you're not in that position, you're not pushing yourself enough."

Ali, Events Company Founder

"There's tons of stuff you won't know. You need to learn fast and be smart about how you allocate time to that, because you can't possibly do everything. Research topics you have no clue about, just get into it and start gaining an understanding. For example in my business, I had no experience of dealing with suppliers - you start making calls, you ask all the dumb questions, and eventually you start asking smart questions! You really have to push yourself to do things you're uncomfortable with."

Alessa, Business Founder

"It takes a lot of energy, determination and stamina. Each step takes time. It's not passion you need, it's perseverance."

Tamsin, Jewellery Business Founder

85

FURTHER STUDY

Postgraduate qualifications

Around a fifth of graduates end up going onto part or full-time further study. Postgraduate study may enhance your career prospects and earnings potential, as well as personal development. But it will require planning and preparation and you should make sure you pursue further study for the right reasons.

A master's can provide an opportunity to specialise and develop expertise in a particular subject, or to change career direction (e.g. conversion courses). For some professions, a relevant postgraduate qualification is mandatory e.g. law, education, architecture and certain areas of healthcare. For other careers, the extra academic qualification could give you a competitive edge, but bear in mind, it won't be a game changer for all vocations. Some employers would prefer to see real industry experience over an extra qualification.

Be clear how you expect a postgraduate qualification to help you achieve your goals. You need to weigh up the time commitment, intense effort, cost and value of further study against the insight and expertise you would gain from the extra months or years of work.

If you're self-funding your studies, always check if you qualify for a bursary, scholarship, grant or loan.

Short courses

You could select from a wide variety of free or lower-cost short courses, many of which can be done online or fitted into evenings around work. Not only can learning or training boost your career prospects, the challenge will help keep you motivated during your job search and demonstrate to employers that you are ambitious, hardworking and keen to learn. And you'll feel more fulfilled, too. There are hundreds of short course providers, offering courses of varying quality. Always do your research to find out what qualifications are most coveted and respected in the industry or specialism you'd like to work in.

Alessa taught herself topics ranging from biotech to cryptocurrencies, which all supported her journey as an entrepreneur and investor:

"Treat learning as a never-ending process. Be curious. Expand your comfort zone. Inform yourself, learn new skills. Don't think that it's like at uni where you go to a class and get taught something. It's much more exciting than that because it's up to you. Having that curious attitude where you want to discover and explore what is out there is great, and it's fun!"

"Continuous learning is one of the most important elements for being successful in life. Once you've gone through uni, the idea of further studying may not appeal, you might not want to take any more exams, but read a book on something you'd like to learn about. There are some fantastic business books that shed new light, new info. If you're up with the latest information, that's always going to help in whatever you're doing, and to be constantly growing is really important for personal fulfilment."

Claire, Business Coach

86

GO ABROAD TO WORK, STUDY OR TRAVEL

While you're young and free of commitments, exploring more of the world is a realistic goal. You could travel to immerse yourself in different cultures, or have a more specific aim in mind, e.g. to become fluent in another language. It may also give you time to reflect on your career plans while you gain valuable life experience.

As well as personal enrichment, time spent overseas can also increase your employability. In our global economy, companies value an international outlook and cultural awareness. And, whether you are working abroad, volunteering or studying, international experience demonstrates to potential employers that you are self-motivated, organised, resourceful and able to adapt to change and take on new challenges.

Whatever your plans and budget, you can go it alone or you'll find plenty of business and charitable organisations who run work, study and volunteer programmes. The opportunities are endless: you could teach English as a foreign language, work with children, assist with healthcare projects or fieldwork, or find paid work with a body like the British Council. But before you jump on the next flight, do some proper research to make sure you're signing up to work for a reputable organisation.

"IF YOU DON'T YET HAVE ANY INTERNATIONAL, CROSS-CULTURAL EXPERIENCE, I RECOMMEND YOU GET SOME. EITHER LIVE OVERSEAS A WHILE OR WORK IN A MULTINATIONAL ORGANISATION. IMMERSING YOURSELF IN A NEW ENVIRONMENT BUILDS CONFIDENCE AND CAN HELP YOU GROW INTO AN ADAPTABLE, OPEN-MINDED, MORE ROUNDED INDIVIDUAL. HAVING AN APPRECIATION OF OTHER CULTURES, UNDERSTANDING THOSE THAT THINK AND ACT DIFFERENTLY, CREATES A RICHNESS IN PEOPLE."

PETER, BUSINESS CONSULTANT

Off we go!

"Travel is one of the best schools. You'll learn a lot from different environments and pushing yourself out there. It will help shape what you think you want to do. Taking a gap between jobs or after university is absolutely fine as long as it's a constructive, logical course of action. And you only get one life!"

Jill, Sales & Marketing Director (& travel addict!)

CONSIDER A 'CAREER GAP YEAR'

Not sure where to start? If you're confused about your next steps, consider taking a career gap year, or at least a few months, to explore as many different industries as you can, and speak to all kinds of people. Use temp work, shift work, tutoring and freelancing to earn some cash and help you to fund work experience placements, volunteering, further learning and/or travel.

The goal is to end up with a clearer idea of what you enjoy, the way you like to work and fields that interest you. The experiences you gather will make you work-ready, equip you with transferable skills and expand your network, all of which will help with your subsequent job search.

> "Focus on building transferable skills, then you'll be ready for anything. It's even more important in these ever-changing times."
>
> Fraser, Digital Strategist

* Gain a clearer idea of what you enjoy

WORRIED ABOUT YOUR UNIVERSITY GRADES?

If you got a 2:2 or a third, you're in excellent company, joining the likes of Countdown maths whizz Carol Vorderman, best-selling authors AA Milne and JK Rowling, broadcaster David Dimbleby, and adventurer Bear Grylls, to name but a few.

Plenty of companies don't request high grades, and plenty employ people who don't have degrees. Employers are increasingly scrutinising their hiring policies because personality fit, how you approach tasks, solve problems and how your brain works are actually better indicators of how you'll perform and fit in.

So, while some entry-level jobs and grad schemes do have minimum degree requirements, it's certainly not the case for every employer.

If you're disappointed with your grade, don't worry. As long as you're positive and proactive, you can make good things happen. Here's how...

Be prepared to take a **less direct route** into your preferred career and be open to roles with less demanding entry requirements such as recruitment, sales or admin. If you can get a foot in the door, build experience and prove yourself, you may be able to transfer to a different role later.

SMEs and startups are a great option, because in a small workforce, cultural fit and attitude will be as least as important as your degree grade. So, do your research and send off a tailored speculative application, ensuring your personality shines through and explaining how you would be a great fit for the company.

Find ways to stand out. Many companies make decisions based on the strength of a showstopping cover letter, or a truly creative or unique application. Work on your CV to highlight non-academic attributes and skills that make you an ideal candidate e.g. extracurricular activities, volunteering, and temp work.

Research **short courses and qualifications** specific to your industry or career to boost employability and demonstrate determination. Likewise, read everything you can so your knowledge of new trends, technology and techniques is razor sharp. Show off your new knowledge by posting about it on LinkedIn.

Focus on securing **work experience and internships**. You will definitely accumulate new skills and you may be able to impress them enough to be offered a permanent position. If not, named placements will set you apart in future job applications because employers will view you as being 'work ready'.

Use your **network** (personal and professional) to talk to people in industry, join discussions, find out what's going on, ask pertinent questions, and make yourself visible. Remember a high proportion of positions are filled through networking.

And remember, there will come a time in your career when no one bothers to ask about your degree any more.

"My advice for anyone who hasn't got the best academic marks would be to do a job that gets you over that, so you can say now I have experience.

Aim for the best you can, but if you don't get it straight away, don't despair. Take second best, reassess and stick at it, and it might turn out to be brilliant! Or be prepared to move on."

Monica, Business Adviser

HOW TO CHOOSE THE RIGHT CAREER & COMPANY

If you're heading down the right career path, and you've found a workplace with a culture that fits, you're more likely to be engaged, happy and fulfilled by what you do every day. This section is dedicated to helping you do exactly that. By the time you've read it, and taken our quiz, you should have a clearer picture of what the future holds. And even if that's not the case, your brain will begin mulling it over... promise!

> DON'T WORRY IF YOU DON'T LOVE YOUR FIRST JOB, IF YOU'RE LEARNING AND DEVELOPING. CAREER PATHS ARE NOT A STRAIGHT LINE. AS LONG AS YOU'RE COMFORTABLE THAT IT'S PUTTING YOU ON THE RIGHT PATH, AND YOU'RE STEPPING CLOSER TO YOUR DESTINATION, ALTHOUGH YOU MIGHT DEVIATE, JUST GET IN THERE AND SEE WHAT HAPPENS.

PATRICK, MENTOR &
BUSINESS ADVISER

CAREER DIRECTION:
What do you want to do?

The dreaded question! Some of you will have a vocational degree and a predetermined career path in a field like medicine, veterinary science or law, but many more leave university without any clear career direction. It's perfectly OK to not know what you want to do yet.

One piece of career advice we hear over and over is to 'do something you're passionate about'. If you're lucky enough to have a passion that can earn you a living, that's fantastic! At the other end of the spectrum are those people who take a job just for the salary, which enables them to pursue a passion outside of work, be it cycling, mountain climbing, surfing or photography.

But for most people, the solution is not quite so cut and dried. Then the key is to explore areas that spark your interest. Passion is something that can evolve with experience and, if you begin with a genuine curiosity, you're more likely to grow to love what you're doing and make a success of it.

Don't be seduced into a job just because it sounds impressive, pays well or fits what you think you ought to be doing. And don't feel pressured by comparisons with friends, or what family members expect. It's OK to be different. Be comfortable pursuing what feels right for you and only you.

If you try something, and you're not sure how long to stick it out for, one sterling piece of advice is this: never quit on a bad day. Pick the 'wrong' path now or make a 'bad' decision, and you've got decades to correct it. As a person in your 20s, you shouldn't feel any pressure to find the perfect job. First of all, it's unlikely to exist. Second, career development is an ongoing process that's full of change. Any job might even open doors in unexpected ways, through meeting useful contacts or learning new skills, so just have a go!

"How do you want to make a difference in the world? Where do you think you can add real value? We all have to earn money to keep body and soul together and satisfy our basic needs, but it's so much better if it's in an area you feel passionate about; it gives you a lot of interest and excitement. Also, I assume it stands to reason that if you're highly motivated about something you will be better at it. So, make a conscious effort to try and work that out."

Jon, British Diplomat

STARTING POINTS FOR CONTEMPLATING YOUR CAREER DIRECTION

Time for a short quiz! While this is by no means conclusive or exhaustive, it might help you understand your priorities so you can shortlist some roles and industries to look at. Here we go!

1. What was your favourite thing about going to university?

A) I met so many interesting people
B) I got grades I could be proud of
C) I learned so much
D) I earned respect
E) I got to work on what I liked

2. What would you be most proud to achieve at the end of a working day?

A) I helped someone, even in just a small way
B) I figured out a solution that had been bugging people for weeks
C) I wrote something that I thought was of high quality
D) I did something entirely on my own and it succeeded
E) I made something interesting

3. Which one of these statements is MOST important to you?

A) I want to work face-to-face with people
B) I don't mind working at a desk, but I want a team to work with
C) I need deadlines and structure to do my best work
D) I want control of my work and to be able to call it mine
E) I need to work somewhere I can express myself

4. Computers?

A) Never the most interesting part of a job
B) Tech has always been a hobby
C) I'm no tech-whiz, but I always need to stay up-to-date and available so I'm never far from a machine
D) A necessary tool to get a job done and I'm comfortable working all-day on one
E) I don't necessarily want to work at a desk all day, but I'm pretty good on a lot of different programs

5. What is my top skill?

A) Empathy
B) Attention to detail
C) Communication
D) Leadership
E) Creativity

6. Which of the following best describes your outlook on work?

A) I want to make a difference to people's lives
B) I want to work towards goals and know that I'm getting there
C) I don't want to do the same thing every day
D) I want to work on something that is truly my own
E) I like to find new ways of doing things

7. What are your thoughts on money?

A) It isn't what drives me
B) A good salary is a big consideration for me
C) Money motivates me, so I would be driven by bonuses for good performance
D) I would like to live comfortably and that is what work is for
E) Money is a good reward, but not the sole purpose of my career

8. Where would you like to work?

A) I wouldn't want to be on my own the whole time
B) An office is fine
C) I'd like to change things up and work from different places
D) I need control over my workspace, so in my own space or at home
E) Not too fussed, it is has never been much of an issue as long as I have what I need

Mostly As: The Helper

You probably aren't interested in 'big business' and the whole rat race to success. Consider looking at roles where you can make a tangible, one-to-one impact on people's lives or just something where you know you are making a difference to people.

Check out: Third sector jobs (charities, NGOs etc), carer, teacher, healthcare and social enterprises or B-corp certified businesses, which balance profit with purpose.

Mostly Bs: The Problem Solver

You've always had an eye for detail and you rely on your analytical skills, determination, resilience and/or intuition to complete tasks. You are probably comfortable working alone or in a team as long as you are working towards getting the job done.

Interested in tech? Check out: Software development, coding, systems analyst, data engineer, design, scientist
Not interested in tech? Check out: Actuary, accounting, consulting, copywriter, editor

Mostly Ds: The Freelancer/Entrepreneur

More than anything, you want to find your own path. This doesn't mean you never should work for other people, but that isn't your end goal. You might be interested in management, freelancing in a certain field or attempting to start your own business.

This will require hard work and a solid network of mentors and advisers to help you get going, as well as cash reserves, but ultimately you want to work for yourself.

Mostly Es: The Creative

You want to do something interesting, exciting and innovative and the idea of trawling through spreadsheets and paperwork sends shivers down your spine. Creative roles aren't limited to the arts and design. Take a look at tech, retail and media where you can also find opportunities to flex your creative muscles.

Check out: Web design, graphic design, UX, crafts, theatre set design, broadcast, production, journalist, writer, product design, service design

Mostly Cs: The Learner

Not every job is about repetitive tasks and you probably need a role that stretches you, if you are to stay motivated. You might be surprised at how many things can keep you feeling sharp and driven and not like a worker drone. Some jobs involve learning and adapting to constantly changing situations and while they might not all interest you, some definitely will.

Check out: Technology, science, engineering, law, marketing, PR, journalism, sales

PERSONALITY QUESTIONNAIRES & PSYCHOMETRIC TESTS

We all make assumptions about our own abilities, but psychometric tests and personality questionnaires can help us learn more about ourselves and direct us towards careers that are likely to be a good fit. Because they help map strengths, weaknesses, aptitudes, competencies and character, they can also identify interests and values that will be fundamental to job satisfaction.

- **Psychometric tests** give insights on which roles and industries will suit you based on your aptitude and reasoning.

- **Personality questionnaires** analyse typical behaviour by looking at character traits e.g. how you interact with your environment and other people, what motivates you, and your preferred manner of doing things.

There's a wide array of tests available, including many online options. Some charge for their service, others are free, or give you an initial top-line assessment hoping you'll pay for an in-depth report later. Bear in mind that all tests have their limitations, so view them as just one tool in your career planning, and do plenty of other research.

"TRY TO HAVE SOME LEVEL OF SELF-AWARENESS THAT KNOWS WHAT YOU LIKE DOING AND THEN TRY TO LOOK FOR JOBS THAT ALLOW YOU TO DO THAT, IN COMPANIES WHERE THE CULTURE SUITS YOU. BUT DON'T BE AFRAID TO CHANGE, DON'T BE AFRAID TO GRAB NEW OPPORTUNITIES BECAUSE THAT'S HOW YOU LEARN MORE ABOUT YOURSELF. YOU BECOME MORE SELF-AWARE THE OLDER YOU GET AND THE FURTHER YOU GET IN YOUR CAREER AS YOU TRY NEW THINGS."

BRUCE, LEISURE COMPANY CEO

5-Minute Exercise

1. Think of someone you admire and whose career you would LOVE to have.

2. Write down what you like about it, from their lifestyle to their work schedule.

3. Look at that person's career history (try LinkedIn or Wikipedia and press interviews if they're well known) and the steps they took to get there.

Obviously, you should always follow your own path, but sometimes having a look at someone else's blueprint can make everything look a bit more manageable. It could lead you to the perfect master's, an internship or company, or it could just give you an idea of how to get started.

CULTURE IS KING

What is company culture & why does it matter?

Culture is the very 'personality' of an organisation, characterised by its core values, vision, attitudes, communications and much more. It's reflected in the way people behave and work together, where they see the business going and how they are taking it there, and how they interact with the outside world, including their customers.

How well you relate to an organisation's ethos will be directly proportional to your happiness at work, affecting how engaged you feel, your level of job satisfaction, relationships with colleagues and, ultimately, your performance. That's why 'cultural fit' should be a really important consideration when choosing a company. It's equally crucial for employers selecting candidates.

With this in mind, make sure your job applications highlight personal attributes and interests that demonstrate how well you would be suited to the company culture. For example, what is it about your personality that would mean you'd feel right at home in:

- **a hierarchical organisation with a corporate feel**
- **a creative, quirky workplace**
- **an energetic, fast-moving, high pressure environment, where the focus is on meeting deadlines and smashing targets**
- **a relaxed, liberal, informal culture**
- **a role where you work from home full time**

How to find out about company culture before you join

This is really easy to research by reviewing a company's website, blogs, social channels, media coverage, and by looking at its products or services.

What do they post about? How do they engage with customers and employees? What are their workers saying about the company online? How are they perceived by the outside world? What is their online reputation? Check out online forums and employee and customer reviews on sites like Glassdoor and Google.

Try to network with people connected to the organisation via LinkedIn or through any personal contacts. If possible, interact with the company as a customer and jot down some notes about the transaction. If you land a job interview, ask questions about the company culture. You could even ask to be put in touch with an employee who's done your job before.

All these elements will help you decide whether it's likely to be a good fit for your personality, values and ambitions.

"Cultural fit is key. Choose an environment that makes you smile, something that feels positive and worthwhile. It's about following your heart as well as your head."

Jill, Sales & Marketing Director

" Do not underestimate the happiness when you are in a culture that suits you and the complete and utter stress and awfulness if you are in an environment that you don't like. I've done jobs where on the face of it, the product has been lovely and the work hasn't been hard, yet the culture has been difficult and hasn't suited me personally. I've found that really challenging.

You might be seduced by what the company promises you: the money, the car and all the rest. I think you have to learn to cut through some of that and really try to understand what is at the beating heart of this company. What are the people like? What are the senior people like? What do they believe in? What motivates them? And will I be happy there?

So, do your research and talk to people: try to find people who used to work for that company and have left, clients, suppliers, advisers, current employees. Use whatever touch points you can to really see if they reflect what the company is telling you. But, probably more than anything, trust your gut instinct. It is a powerful and well-honed thing. **"**

Bruce,
leisure company CEO

EQUALITY, DIVERSITY & INCLUSION IN THE WORKPLACE

Diversity and inclusion cover race, ethnicity, gender, sexual orientation, age, physical abilities, socio-economics, religious beliefs and other ideologies.

"Inclusion is where people's differences are valued and used to enable everyone to thrive at work. ... An inclusive workplace has fair policies and practices in place and enables a diverse range of people to work together effectively."

CIPD Chartered Institute of Personnel and Development

What is the reality for jobseekers today, and what should candidates expect from employers when it comes to equality, fairness and inclusion?

We spoke to employment lawyer Charlene Brown, a founding partner of Howlett Brown, who has over a decade of experience working on cases involving bullying, harassment and discrimination, whistleblowing, culture, diversity and inclusion. Charlene also delivers training to companies on diversity and inclusion, race and ethnicity, intersectionality, and other protected characteristics in the workplace.

She says: "Deciding where to work is a two-way street, both for you and the prospective employer. You have a lot more say in the matter than you realise. It's important that before you make a decision about where to work, you take steps to understand the workplace culture and the opportunities that might be available to you, how those are offered and what processes a company has in place to make sure there is equity of opportunity internally.

"A lot of companies now have a greater awareness of systemic inequalities, bias and microaggressions that exist in the workplace but there is a lot of work to do to truly improve companies. That is the reality. But many are now taking steps to improve their workplace culture which includes their hiring practices and procedures."

Charlene's top recommendations are:

1. Understand the culture of the company you may decide to join as best as you can. Check out services like Glassdoor which include staff reviews to gain greater insights. If the culture of a workplace doesn't align to your values and what you want for your career, do not accept an offer. If you realise this when you are already at the company, don't hang around for longer than serves you.

2. Take steps to understand the policies, who to contact and where to raise concerns if you identify processes or procedures that are unclear or you think may not be as fair as they appear to be. Leverage internal staff networks within companies for greater support and advocacy.

3. Develop your influence and strategic skills in a way that stays true to who you are as a person and deploy these skills not only in your technical role but also for your career and the way you build business relationships.

See p.95 on how to find out about a company's culture. Careers and education expert, Nicholas Wyman, suggests important things to look out for: "Does the company foreground equality, fairness, and inclusion on their website and how? Or is it just buried in their blog posts? Have they won any awards, maybe been quoted in high-authority publications about their diversity and inclusion achievements? What does their organisational chart look like – is it representative of contemporary society?"

Useful resources

Search online for helpful organisations relevant to your profession or situation. Joining a network can be a great way to make connections, share information and find support.

The Employment Network for Equality & Inclusion represents over 300 employers who are committed to equality and diversity in their organisations **enei.org.uk**

Inclusive Companies shares best practice and drives inclusion, with initiatives such as the National Diversity Awards and The Inclusive Top 50 UK Employers List **inclusivecompanies.co.uk**

VERCIDA, which stands for Values, Equality, Respect, Culture, Inclusion, Diversity, Accessibility, is a platform that aims to connect diverse talent with inclusive employers. As well as a jobs board and info, you'll find a directory of support organisations **vercida.com/uk**

Black Young Professionals Network (BYP) is for new graduates and experienced hires, and includes a dedicated careers site **byp-network.com**

Stonewall produces an annual list of the top 100 most inclusive employers for LGBT **stonewall.org.uk**

Disability Rights offers advice and information including on career opportunities, getting work, education and skills **disabilityrightsuk.org**

THE JOB SEARCH: WHERE TO FIND OPPORTUNITIES

The all-important question now is: where should I be looking for a job? There are plenty of ways to find out about opportunities beyond the well-publicised vacancies. We'll show you where to look and why it's worth adopting a varied job search strategy.

YOUR JOB SEARCH:
eight ways to find opportunities

1 JOBS BOARDS

Including Adzuna, Bright Network, CV-Library, Graduate Jobs, Graduate Recruitment Bureau, Indeed, LinkedIn, Milkround, Monster, Prospects, Reed, Target Jobs, The Dots and TotalJobs.

2 COMPANY WEBSITES

Look for 'work with us' or 'careers' sections, or read company blogs to find vacancies.

3 RECRUITMENT SERVICES

- Recruitment agencies match suitable candidates to jobs. Some specialise in placing graduates or only work with certain industries.

- Lists of top graduate recruiters: The Times Top 100 Graduate Employers is probably the best known

"I realised at university that my passion was all about food. I loved going around supermarkets. But I wasn't sure what aspect I wanted to work in. So my entry point was to look at retailers and what graduate schemes were available. Reading The Times Top 100 Graduate Employers list was a great place to start."

Rebecca, joined the Tesco food buying grad scheme and is now a food product developer

Tip
Recruiters and headhunters work on commission so – once they've placed a candidate in a job – they normally take a generous fee from the company they've been instructed by. Don't ever feel pressured into applying for or accepting a job if it doesn't feel right for you.

4 SOCIAL HIRING

Many employers now use their websites and social media to showcase their culture and attract jobseekers. So follow companies you'd like to work for and look out for advertised vacancies, industry networking events and company news that could lead to hiring opportunities. Join forums and discussions to increase your visibility.

6 SPECULATIVE APPLICATIONS

Some businesses will consider candidates who have directly approached them, even if there's no advertised vacancy. And it shows initiative and enthusiasm. Tell them why you'd be a great fit and why you'd love to work for them.

8 NEWS SOURCES

Keep your finger on the pulse of business developments that could lead to hiring: acquisitions and mergers, company expansions, firms that have landed big contracts, launched a successful new product/service or ventured into new geographical markets. If you see an opportunity, fire off a speculative application.

5 NETWORKING

- Tell friends and family what you're looking for – they might know people who can help.

- Your uni or college should have an alumni careers support service, and you can keep in touch with tutors.

- Real or virtual careers fairs and industry events aren't just for students. Go prepared with your 'elevator pitch', pertinent questions for employers and printed copies of your CV.

- You can approach industry professionals on LinkedIn with connection requests accompanied by polite messages.

7 WORK EXPERIENCE & INTERNSHIPS

For many employers, placements form part of the recruitment process. Perform well and you could be offered a permanent role, or be top of the list when an opening does occur.

LIFE ISN'T A RACE

No need to rush, success can come at any age!
People who peaked later in life:

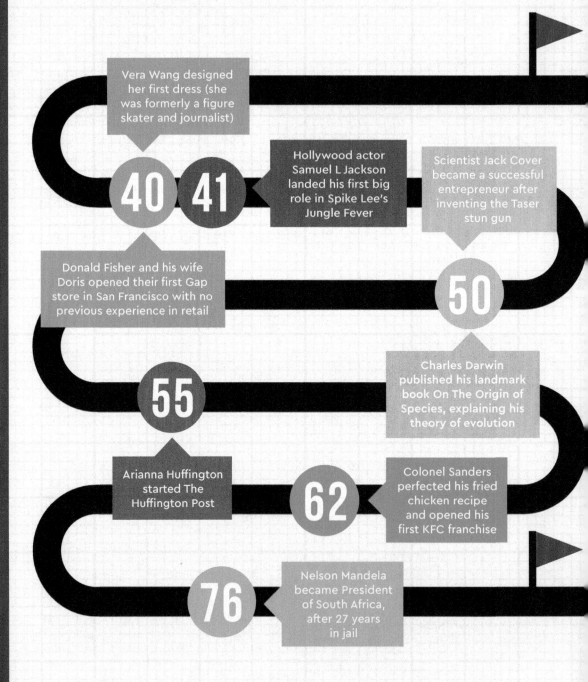

Vera Wang designed her first dress (she was formerly a figure skater and journalist)

Hollywood actor Samuel L Jackson landed his first big role in Spike Lee's Jungle Fever

Scientist Jack Cover became a successful entrepreneur after inventing the Taser stun gun

40 41

Donald Fisher and his wife Doris opened their first Gap store in San Francisco with no previous experience in retail

50

Charles Darwin published his landmark book On The Origin of Species, explaining his theory of evolution

55

Arianna Huffington started The Huffington Post

Colonel Sanders perfected his fried chicken recipe and opened his first KFC franchise

62

Nelson Mandela became President of South Africa, after 27 years in jail

76

Summing Up

Finding your first graduate job can be tough. You will have to be persistent and resourceful and may need to try various different approaches. Where you are unsuccessful, learn from the experience, try to remain positive and resilient. It is often a numbers game, but you will get there!

There are plenty of routes you can take after university and everyone's journey is different. Whatever you choose to do now, it is not a lifetime commitment. These days, careers are much more fluid and flexible, and you might change tack several times over the course of your working life. So, don't worry if you're unsure about your career direction and don't fret about finding the perfect job. Think about what you would like to do for the next few years, and just give it a go!

"Take your time to reflect, think about what has gone well and what hasn't, think about what you might like to do; you don't have to have all the answers now. You don't need to find a job that ticks all the boxes now, you are going to be learning throughout your life. But if there is something you're really passionate about, get out there and do it. "

Chloë, Early Careers Coach

6

JOB HUNTING:
HOW TO STAND
Out

This chapter covers all you need to know about applying for jobs. We'll discuss what employers typically look for, then show you how to impress at every opportunity, from writing a polished CV and online profile, to sailing through tests, nailing interviews and dealing with job offers.

PREPARATION

Before you start applying for jobs, it's time to get organised.

You want to be ready to pounce on any great opportunities, but also be well prepared for recruiters scouting for talent. It means presenting your best (professional) self and there's a logical order to doing this: first, understand what employers look for and how you can add value, then set about creating your CV and perfecting your online profile.

What do employers look for?

There's plenty of research you can do to build an understanding of what hard skills are most valued by companies in the industries that appeal to you. Then there are general employability skills and traits – so-called 'soft skills' – that can make you more attractive to recruiters and hiring managers.

A recent survey found that whilst a strong academic record is a plus, most employers regard 'aptitude and readiness for work' as the key consideration when hiring education leavers. And 60% rated broad 'soft' skills as a top priority (e.g. problem-solving, communication, teamwork, adaptability and resilience).

CBI.org.uk

What does this mean for jobseekers?

Depending on the role, you may need evidence of specific 'technical' skills or academic qualifications. But, in general, employers are looking for well-rounded individuals who are team players, who demonstrate a positive attitude and the soft skills that are so needed in companies.

Think about what you can offer an employer. As a new graduate, you won't have much of an employment history, but you can certainly draw on experience outside the world of work to demonstrate you have these valued transferable skills and personal qualities: from your studies, extra-curricular activities, personal interests, sports and travel, as well as any volunteering, internships or previous jobs.

Most employers know the value of creating an inclusive workplace, and will be keen to attract diverse talent, recognising that employees from different backgrounds bring unique skills and knowledge. Teams are known to be strengthened by diversity, increasing creative flow, innovation, customer insights etc. So, what's unique about you, your background, your lived experience, or how you approach problems that could be a strength and asset in the workplace?

Work out how best to communicate those attributes in a positive way that is relevant to the business you're applying to. Show how your experience has given you some valuable perspectives e.g. an understanding of a culturally diverse customer base, new ways of thinking, resilience and determination, adaptability, empathy. Be proud of who you are.

 YOU DON'T HAVE TO TICK ALL THE BOXES TO GET A JOB, PARTICULARLY AS A NEW GRADUATE, YOU WON'T HAVE A LOT OF EXPERIENCE. REMEMBER EMPLOYERS ARE BUYING INTO YOU, NOT JUST YOUR SKILLS.

JILL, SALES & MARKETING DIRECTOR

CV 101

Your CV provides a brief overview of your education, qualifications, skills and experience. Given that hiring managers will generally scan a CV in 30 seconds to decide whether you might fit the bill, you'll need that document to make an immediate and lasting impact!

It's fine to use sample CVs as a guide, but don't just complete an online template – that won't impress. Instead, use these guidelines to create your own.

Consider any industry-specific requirements, because whilst the general approach will be the same, they can vary significantly in terms of length, layout and emphasis. For example, creative industries may appreciate an original design element; a technical CV often starts with a paragraph about your technical expertise and key skills; whilst an academic CV is longer and very comprehensive, focusing on educational achievements and research interests.

1. START BY WRITING A MASTER CV

Create a master document recording everything you've done, including qualifications, skills and experience. Note dates and company details as well as what you achieved and learned. This is the time-consuming part, but you'll then be ready to simply tweak it, to present the strongest version for every job you apply for.

2. DEMONSTRATE GOOD COMMUNICATION SKILLS

- Your CV must be well presented, clear and concise, without spelling mistakes or poor grammar.

- Keep it short: maximum two pages (one page for financial CVs, and often longer for medical or academic CVs so check the norm for your industry).

3. WHAT TO INCLUDE

NAME

Make your name stand out on the page.

CONTACT DETAILS

Address, email, phone number and links to any professional social media or relevant online presence e.g. LinkedIn, Twitter, portfolio, blog, website.

OPENING STATEMENT/ PERSONAL PROFILE (optional)

Your elevator pitch (a succinct and persuasive sales pitch) outlining who you are, your accomplishments and how they will benefit the business you're applying to. This should be no more than a couple of short sentences.

There are differing views on whether to include an introductory statement: some recruiters say it tends to oversell, which puts them off, others say it grabs the attention and helps them decide whether to read on, while some industries specifically request one.

If you do open with a short statement, make sure it's engaging, well written and doesn't just repeat information you've included further down in your CV.

PROFESSIONAL EXPERIENCE

Paid employment, internships, work experience, voluntary jobs.

Put these in reverse chronological order (most recent first). Include dates, employer, job title and your main duties (do expand on relevant tasks to demonstrate what you actually accomplished).

Provide evidence from your experience that you meet the job requirements:

- Qualities and skills specific to the role
- General employability skills
- Show what you could contribute by describing your achievements using STAR: Situation, Task, Action, Result

QUALIFICATIONS & ACHIEVEMENTS

Languages, scholarships, certificates, proficiency in computer programmes, training courses you have attended etc.

EDUCATION

University/college and secondary education only. In reverse chronological order (most recent first). Give dates, name of institution, qualifications.

INTERESTS

Don't underestimate the importance of non-academic achievements and activities. These add a personal touch, show you're well-rounded, and could be the differentiating factor (particularly at graduate level when applicants have limited experience of the workplace), because employers will hire people they can relate to, and who would gel with their team. The fact that you're a keen photographer, help out in your community, or play football for your local team might just seal the deal!

Describing your interests in a way that highlights personal development, responsibility or relevant skills can give you that extra edge:

- Team sports demonstrate commitment, discipline, responsibility, energy, enthusiasm and working with others
- Volunteer work could show initiative, social interaction and leadership
- Music, art and drama portray creativity, focus, dedication and passion

4. BE YOURSELF

- Your CV should reflect your personality. Tell the truth and write in a way that makes you feel comfortable, avoiding clichés.

- Emphasise your strengths and achievements, using positive, assertive terms e.g. 'adapted', 'developed', 'organised', 'resolved'. Sell yourself!

- No need to state the obvious e.g. if you got top grades throughout school and university, there's no need to mention you're results-driven.

5. TAILOR YOUR CV TO EACH JOB APPLICATION

You will need to customise your master CV, to address the employer's requirements and show how you meet them. Include keywords from the job description (which will also get your CV ranked higher by automated applicant tracking systems). Highlight your most relevant strengths and accomplishments to illustrate how you could add value to the business and would fit in well. (See how to tailor your application on p.120).

6. ADDRESS GAPS

Unexplained gaps will only raise questions. So, if there are certain periods when you were neither working nor studying, give reasons and talk up the skills and experience you gained instead.

7. UPDATE REGULARLY

As you accumulate experience, replace earlier or less relevant parts of your CV with better examples. Always submit a CV that is fully up-to-date.

Chris Matchan, HR professional, explains three things he looks for in a CV: scale, complexity and track record.

1 "What is the <u>scale</u> of what you have done? You might be a grad with little work experience, but perhaps you have been part of a project team – was that two or 20 people? If you had a Saturday job, was it with Dixons or the corner shop?

2 "<u>Complexity</u>: was the stuff you've done dead easy or quite demanding? If you have no work experience, tell me how difficult your degree was.

3 "Show your <u>track record</u>: what were your grades for your degree and A-Levels? Did you pass first time in your professional exams?"

VIDEO CV

Video CVs are becoming popular to enhance an application, particularly where good presentation skills are key, like creative or customer-facing roles in advertising, PR, sales, marketing or media.

Tackle your video CV in the same professional manner you would approach an interview. The video should last between one and three minutes, allowing you to introduce yourself and explain why you're the right candidate for the job, while ensuring your personality shines through.

Bear in mind that a poorly produced video could risk recruiters rejecting you before they have even met you but, if you are adept at communicating what you have to offer, then the addition of a video CV could give you the edge.

SOCIAL MEDIA –
PERFECT YOUR PROFILE

Social media is widely used to attract, find and vet talent. Your online profile could be the first thing a prospective employer sees of you, so make sure it strengthens rather than sabotages your chances! A smart social profile is just as important as a slick CV.

Professional profile

LinkedIn is the leading channel for social hiring; find out on p. 112 how to make your profile an employer magnet. Also set up a professional profile on any other space that's appropriate for your career path, for example:

- **Instagram** is the go-to for creatives, providing an attractive (and free) way to digitally display your portfolio.

- **Twitter** is super important for the arts and journalism, and is also popular for tech, finance and retail.

- In many cases, it helps to create your own **website or blog**, which can be done easily and cheaply on sites like Wordpress or Wix.

Personal profile

A good professional image is only part of the picture. Hiring managers may check any public personal social media accounts like Facebook, Snapchat and Instagram as a way to vet you.

Posting about your passions and interests shows you're social, communicative and have a life outside work. But tighten privacy settings and remove (or make private) anything that could be seen as unprofessional. Google your name to see what comes up – whatever you find, an employer can find too!

Choose a sensible email address based on your first and last names (not the comedy one you set up when you were 14!)

Social Dos & Don'ts

Four out of five employers say they have rejected candidates based on social media content.

Most common reasons for rejecting a candidate

- ✗ Alcohol or drug habits
- ✗ Badmouthing an employer/employee
- ✗ Inappropriate photos
- ✗ Sexual posts
- ✗ Spelling & grammar
- ✗ Bad language or discriminatory comments
- ✗ Lying about qualifications

Reasons why a profile conveyed a good impression

- ✓ Appealing, well-rounded <u>personality</u>
- ✓ <u>Professional</u> image
- ✓ Good <u>communication</u> skills
- ✓ Supported <u>qualifications,</u> or included favourable <u>references</u> posted by others
- ✓ Showed <u>creativity</u>

How to wow with LinkedIn®

Your LinkedIn profile acts as an online CV, so it needs to be complete and polished. But whilst your CV is formal, your LinkedIn profile can have more of a social (though still professional) tone. And, as well as showing what you have achieved so far, it also lets people know your career aspirations, provides an opportunity to showcase your work, and gives a glimpse of your personality.

First impressions are important, so pay particular attention to your photo, headline and summary.

1. Photo

Profiles with a photo get around 20 times more views and, more importantly, you'll increase the credibility of your profile, meaning people are more likely to accept when you send invitations to connect with them. Include a quality headshot taken in good lighting that strikes the right balance between professional and friendly.

2. Headline

In the place of a job title, add a very short summary to explain what you can offer. Give people a reason to click 'connect'. e.g. Bristol marketing graduate with work experience. Creative thinker, keen to work in advertising.

Name Surname
Headline
500 connections

Open to · Add section · M...

> TIP: Search LinkedIn for people doing the job you want and use their headline as a guide to create your own.

About

+ Add summary

3. Summary or About

Think of this section as an elevator pitch that lets people know what you're about. In a few succinct paragraphs, highlight your talents and what you love doing, and where you want to go next.

Unlike your CV which should be tailored to every job you apply for, your LinkedIn summary needs to speak to a broader audience yet be specific enough to show up in search results.

Experience

 Experience 1

Experience 2

Education

Education 1

 Education 2

4. Words matter

Choose your vocabulary carefully. Overused words like 'confident' or 'enthusiastic' are simply less memorable while descriptors like 'experienced' and 'accomplished' are inappropriate coming from a new graduate. Instead, show off your creativity by selecting words that still fit, but that are less often used, such as: 'assertive', 'articulate', 'perceptive', 'composed', 'droll', 'prudent'.

Workplace

University

TIP: Use keywords

Many large companies use scanning software known as applicant tracking systems (ATS) to filter LinkedIn profiles/ CVs/applications, before they ever get seen by a human. So, when describing your skills, include industry keywords that feature in job specifications, to ensure the tracking system ranks you higher up the list of suitable candidates.

5. Experience and Education

In these two sections, relevance is key. Rather than just listing your education or employment history, present your strengths and skills and how you made a contribution.

As a recent graduate with little career experience, it can be helpful to include other things that are relevant to your professional aspirations such as degree modules, dissertation, projects, volunteering, societies, qualifications and other achievements.

Use bullet points to help readers quickly scan the content.

6. Showcase your work

You can attach media to your Summary, Experience and Education sections, including documents, videos and photos. Use this as your portfolio for prospective employers and upload the best projects you've worked on. (Note that you may need client permission to share). If you're not in a creative field, you could add slide decks, PDFs and case studies for added profile flair.

7. Additional Information

Either here, or in your summary, share your passions outside work, and how they have helped cultivate transferable skills or personal qualities.

8. Personalise your URL

Replace the default version with a customised URL to improve your search results (plus it looks better on emails and business cards). **https://www.linkedin. com/in/namesurname/**

Add Experience

Headline

Industry*

LinkedIn uses industry information to provide more relevant recommendations

Description

Media

Add or link to external documents, photos, sites, videos, and presentations.

+ Add media

9. Endorsements and Recommendations

These two important sections allow for other people to vouch for your skills and experience, increasing your credibility for prospective employers and strengthening your LinkedIn profile.

List skills relevant to your chosen career and ask people you have worked with to endorse them (they can do this with one click). Endorsements increase the likelihood of being discovered for openings related to your abilities. Search engines and tracking systems recognise these skills as 'keywords'.

Past employers and managers can also write you recommendations (testimonials) which will be visible on your profile. Try to get at least a couple, as employers view them as job references.

Skills & Endorsements

View pending endorsements

Skill 1

 Endorsed by John Smith and 2 others who are highly skilled at this

Skill 2

 Endorsed by Jane Doe and 1 other who is highly skilled at this

10. Manage your account and privacy settings

For job hunters, one of the most useful settings that allows you to show recruiters you're actively seeking work is 'open to new opportunities'. You can indicate what work you're interested in and, if you are currently employed, you can still search without alerting your employer.

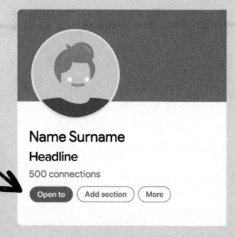

You can also control what parts of your profile are made public, choose to view other people's profiles anonymously and manage notifications so you receive alerts for messages or invitations to connect.

SOCIAL MEDIA: A POWER TOOL FOR JOBSEEKERS

Once you have a strong profile, clever use of social media can give you a competitive edge. (See how to use LinkedIn for networking, p.148)

 Attract employers: maintain an active presence with regular status updates that showcase your work and share your successes.

 Grow and engage with your network: join industry groups, voice your views on current trends and topics, seek help and advice with your career.

 Job search: find opportunities through advertised vacancies and networking.

 Research for applications and interviews: learn about industry news, companies and key people.

JOB APPLICATIONS

Your CV and social profiles are sorted, and you've got a shortlist of jobs that appeal to you. The next step is to wow recruiters with your application.

Successful applications take time and effort. We'll cover some essential general tips and how to ace every step of the graduate job selection process:

Online application
(including cover letter, CV and psychometric tests if required)
Interviews
(which may be by telephone, video or face-to-face)
Assessment centre
(usually comprising a range of individual and group tasks)

Do check specific requirements for your industry or profession.

Planning & Preparation

First, check what is involved in the application process, noting any deadlines. Don't risk leaving it to the last minute or you might miss out. Some graduates have found out the hard way that job opportunities may close early if they've already had a huge response.

Allow plenty of time to research and prepare for each stage, which will boost your confidence and performance.

Keep track of your applications to avoid confusion. Note what stage you have reached, key dates, contacts and any important points to remember.

Sample Applications Tracker

	Company	Role	Date applied	Latest update	Round 1	Round 2
Example	GoldRock	Graduate Scheme	1st January	6th March	Online application / Success	Phone interview / Success
Example	Credit Chase	Financial Analyst	30th January	10th March	Speculative application / Success	Phone interview / Success

keep track of your applications

Action Plan

- [ ] **Check the application process**, noting key dates.

- [ ] **Research** the role, employer, industry and key people.

- [ ] Fine-tune your **CV** and **cover letter**.

- [ ] Plan answers to **online applications**.

- [ ] **Psychometric tests:** find out which system is used and practise tests to improve your scores.

- [ ] **Interviews:** anticipate questions and plan structured answers to include your key selling points. Prepare questions to ask. Practise!

- [ ] **Assessment centres:** find out which tasks the employer uses and practise them.

- [ ] **Follow up** interviews with personalised thanks.

Round 3	Round 4	Offer?	Hiring Manager	Contact details	Notes
Assessment centre	Interview				Interviews 24–26 March
Pending ▾	Select ▾				
Video interview	Assessment centre	N	Mark Goode	email for feedback mgoode@credit-chase.com	
Success ▾	Rejected ▾				

TIP: Check social media and forums for helpful pointers from employers and graduate trainees on their selection process e.g. examples and tips for psychometric tests, how to prepare for assessment centres, typical interview questions and more.

How to
Stand Out

There is no point firing off loads of vague, generic applications, as employers can spot a lack of passion and effort a mile away.

For every job you apply for, the trick is to show genuine interest and enthusiasm for the specific role and company and prove you are well suited, both professionally and personally.

DO YOUR RESEARCH

Really understand what the employer is looking for

TAILOR YOUR APPLICATION

Show how your strengths, experience and values match their job requirements and culture, and explain what you can bring to the role

DO YOUR RESEARCH

You need to go beyond the basics of browsing the company website. Follow their social channels and read recent press releases and media stories, use your network, join industry groups, and look through trade publications to keep updated.

Research the job, company, industry environment and key people. Find out what the role involves and know exactly what employers are looking for (qualifications, general competencies, specific skills). Understand the company values and culture. Get a grasp of their business, which markets they operate in and their main clients and competitors. Read up on any recent major projects. Think about industry trends and challenges, current affairs and world events, and consider how those might impact the business.

The better you understand the business, the more easily you can pitch yourself as the ideal candidate.

The next section will explain what you need to get across with examples of how to do it.

do your research!

TAILOR YOUR APPLICATION

What to do

Use your research findings to convince the employer on these key points:

- That you have a decent understanding of the business and specific role. It's vital that you can explain **why you want the job.**

- **How your skills, experience and qualifications match** the role you're applying for.

- **Why you are a good fit:** that you understand the company culture and core values, and how they relate to your personality and aspirations.

- And, most importantly, **why the employer should choose you over other candidates.** How you fulfil their needs and how your strengths could benefit their business.

"SHOWING ENTHUSIASM DOESN'T JUST MEAN STATING YOU'RE KEEN ON YOUR APPLICATION. WE WANT TO KNOW WHY YOU'RE INTERESTED. WHY DO YOU WANT TO DO THIS ROLE, AND WHY DO YOU WANT TO DO IT WITH US? WHAT DO YOU HOPE TO ACHIEVE? HOW WILL IT HELP YOU GROW AND DEVELOP? "

ROSS, ENTREPRENEUR

"A worrying number of applicants mention — in both cover letters and in interviews — they want the job 'because the benefits and perks are really good'. While that might be absolutely true, they've missed an opportunity to really impress. Interviewers don't want to hire you to enjoy their perks, they want you to develop in the role so you become of greater value to the business than when you first started. Instead, tell the interviewer how you plan to develop your skills and progress within their company."

Emily, PR Business Owner

How to do it

At every stage of the application process, seize the opportunity to prove you are the best candidate for the job:

- In your cover letter, explain why you're keen to join: **what attracts you to the company and role?**

- Adapt your CV, and link applications and interview responses to the job description. You can use the STAR method (explained on p.122) to emphasise **relevant skills and experience.**

- Draw on highlights from your work, extra-curricular activities and life experience, which will show you're a **well-rounded, interesting person.** Aim to give insights into your character that could set you apart as a great fit with the company culture. For example...

 * If it's an energetic, pressured environment, let them know how you can meet deadlines, thrive in a fast-moving atmosphere and stay calm.

 * In a more laid-back, casual culture, demonstrate that you're a self-starter, capable of completing projects without constant supervision.

 * For an innovative, forward-thinking company, show your creative edge, discuss situations where you did things differently or comment on their ways of working that appeal. Show how you would connect with their team.

- Display **enthusiasm and knowledge** of the business by showing awareness of industry issues and voicing informed opinions.

- Ask **pertinent questions** at interviews: enquire about the impact of global trends or find out more about an aspect of the business that inspires you.

show insights from work, extra-curricular activities & life experience

THE STAR METHOD

This is a simple technique for articulating your competencies, by describing specific examples in a clear, concise way. It's particularly useful for framing skills and experience on your CV or application forms, and for structuring responses to interview questions, such as: *Tell me about a time when... Give an example of... Have you ever...*

S — Situation
Set the context for your story. Outline the project/event/challenge you faced.

T — Task
What was your specific role?

A — Action
Explain what you did and how.

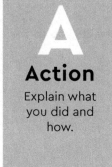

R — Result
Describe what impact you made, providing measurable evidence if possible e.g. benefits, growth, savings, rewards, recognition. Include what you learnt from the situation and if there was anything you would do differently next time.

Example 1

Question:
How do you cope with working under pressure, would you be suited to a fast-moving environment? Give an example of how you have worked to deadlines.

What are they looking for?
- Time management and organisational skills
- Ability to prioritise

Answer:
Situation At university I participated in a 24-hour design competition.

Task The challenge involved working with people from diverse backgrounds who had never met before, to deliver an educational resource for teachers, within an unusually tight timeframe.

Action I led the group by delegating tasks according to individual skills, then set priorities and created a project timeline so we were all aligned and could easily monitor progress. I organised regular updates to keep everyone focused and on track to meet the deadline.

Result I enjoyed the challenge and found I thrived under pressure. I was happy to take control of organising our team, to get the task done well and within the allotted time. We finished with time to spare and were delighted to secure second place in our region.

Other competencies illustrated by this example: teamwork, leadership, motivation, communication skills

Example 2

Question:
Have you ever led a group? How did you approach the situation? What was the outcome?

What are they looking for?
- People skills: leadership, teamwork, motivating others
- Planning and organisation, decision making, problem solving
- Analytical skills: ability to analyse and learn from the experience

Answer:
`Situation` We were doing a group presentation at university and there was a disagreement about what our final recommendations should be.

`Task` I was responsible for writing and presenting our conclusions.

`Action` I listened to everyone's views, weighed up both sides, made my decision and explained it to the group.

`Result` The presentation went well and we were commended for our clear, concise recommendations.

Other competencies illustrated by this example: communication, listening, diplomacy and presentation skills

STAR chart

As part of your jobs prep, make a useful reference document of the key competencies you want to get across in applications and interviews. **But always make sure your responses are tailored to the specific role and company you're applying to.**

Competency	Situation	Task	Action	Result

TIP KEEP YOUR STAR CHART HANDY FOR ONLINE APPLICATIONS AND TELEPHONE OR VIDEO INTERVIEWS, SO YOU CAN QUICKLY REFER TO THE APPROPRIATE QUESTIONS AND ADAPT YOUR RESPONSES ACCORDINGLY.

COVER LETTERS

You will need to write a customised cover letter or email for most types of job application and for making speculative approaches to companies (when you apply directly without waiting for an opening).

Its function is to **introduce you, explain why you're a great fit for the role, and to make recruiters want to meet you.** So, make it meaningful, personal, powerful, and make every sentence count!

Top Tips

- Keep your cover letter short and leave line spaces between paragraphs: a wall of text will instantly turn a reader off.

- It needs to be grammatically perfect and appropriately angled. Take a lead from the company's website and social channels regarding the tone of their communications. Are they corporate and professional, or informal and friendly? Your letter should reflect that tone.

- Good cultural fit is important, so show that you 'get' their business and that your own values and interests echo the company's ethos. Let your personality and passion shine through, to complement your CV (which is a more formal, factual summary of your achievements and experience).

- If you feel passionately about a cause, and you're heavily involved in campaigning or activism, then cultural fit will be even more important. Look for companies with strong values that align with your own and mention this as a talking point in your application.

" Depending on the industry, try to be different if you can. The most creative application I ever received was in a box with stress balls. The cover letter said: "I'm sure you're really busy and quite stressed, so I've sent you some stress balls." That got him an interview in a heartbeat! Just don't look like everybody else, show you've had the nous to try a little bit more. "

Chris, HR Professional

124

HOW TO DO A SPECULATIVE APPROACH

It's well worth applying directly to companies that interest you, even if they are not actively recruiting. This is a particularly effective route into smaller companies, where jobs may not be widely advertised.

A speculative approach should include your CV and a well-crafted cover letter setting out what you are looking for, why you have approached the company and what you can offer.

Top Tips

Follow the previous guidelines for cover letters, but there are a few additional points to note:

- Make it clear what you are looking for: permanent job/internship/work experience.

- When you're not applying for a specific vacancy, it's best to find a 'hook' to explain why you are approaching the company. Perhaps you were inspired by their latest product launch or media campaign. Maybe they share your passion for sustainability, or you heard news of a recent acquisition and thought it might lead to job openings. This sort of targeted approach shows genuine interest and initiative and is more likely to elicit a positive response.

- As with a normal cover letter, explain why you're keen to work for the company, highlighting the relevant skills and experience you'd bring with you.

- Find out the name of the manager responsible for hiring (e.g. the head of department) and send your application directly to them. This is particularly important when applying on spec, as it stands more chance of being read.

- If you haven't heard back, it is worth following up politely after a couple of weeks. But if you still get no response, just move on.

PSYCHOMETRIC TESTING

Psychometric testing is widely used at the initial stage of the screening process, to assess a candidate's competencies, knowledge and personality traits.

Tests can be daunting, especially if you haven't done maths or verbal reasoning since schooldays. But practice makes perfect: it can significantly increase scores. So, find out which system the company uses and practise their tests in advance to improve your speed and accuracy.

APTITUDE TESTS

These are usually timed tests, to evaluate competencies such as numeracy, verbal, spatial and inductive reasoning.

"**To tackle the test:** just crack through it. And don't freak out when you don't finish; you'll rarely finish, but you can still pass the test. Don't agonise over a question you find difficult, leave it or guess. And move on.

"**To improve your scores:** rigorous practice! Repetition makes you get much better because you'll know what to expect, you'll get into a rhythm and you'll feel more confident. So don't let the time you need to be really good at it be your first time - make it your 50th time!"

Chris, HR Professional

PERSONALITY QUESTIONNAIRES

These are used to determine all sorts of character traits, interests, motivations and preferences. Unlike aptitude tests, there are no right or wrong answers – it's more about what part of your brain lights up first.

"There's only one way to do these questionnaires: answer quickly and honestly. They measure personality traits and how people behave in particular situations, they are not skills tests. A recruiter may be looking for someone who enjoys working on their own, or conversely, someone who thrives as part of a team.

"Honesty is important for profiling questionnaires, as it shows the recruiter who you are and how your personality might fit into their business. If you don't get the interview, chances are you wouldn't have been happy in that working environment. There will be others that suit you better!"

Alice, Employment Tests Provider

INTERVIEWS

The next part of the recruitment process is likely to be an interview, either by telephone, video or face-to-face. Here's how to make a great first and lasting impression.

PREPARATION

Good prep is the key to boosting your confidence and putting you at ease, so you can present your best self.

Research

Research the company beyond the basics, refresh your memory by reading the job description and what you wrote in your application.

> **Do your homework, but not to the point where you're worrying about trying to remember things. The interviewer wants to know you've done some research and that you understand the business, but they won't expect you to remember minute details.**
>
> **And it's fine to bring notes into an interview. Do it cleverly, just say 'I hope you don't mind, I've written down some ideas.'**
>
> **Chris, HR professional**

Plan answers to common questions

Most importantly, use your research to explain your motivations for wanting this specific job in this particular organisation and, crucially, why the employer should choose you over other candidates.

Think of the three most important points about yourself you want to get across. These should be relevant attributes or experience that will help you stand out.

"The people who stand out are those who have gone the extra mile in their research. Anyone can look at a company website, so you need to do more. Read the business news, join discussions on social media, understand the industry environment. If it's a service or retailer, try to get customer experience: visit a location or contact a call centre and interact with staff. That'll give a good indication about their culture.

"If you're armed with that extra knowledge, you will feel more confident and that really shows at interviews. It sounds so simple, but it stands out so much."

Jill, Sales & Marketing Director

Use the STAR technique!

127

Anticipate concerns

Be prepared to talk about anything that is likely to raise questions e.g. applying for a role that is unrelated to your degree, gaps in your studies or work, lack of relevant work experience etc. Address it in a positive way, for instance why you're keen to learn.

Prepare questions

Rounding off the interview with a few intelligent questions will show you are serious about the job.

- You could ask what hesitations they might have about hiring you!
- Discover more about the culture by asking 'How do you take care of your employees?' And 'What steps has the business taken to create a positive working environment?'
- Demonstrate your knowledge by enquiring about specific challenges facing the business.

"I was told that I'd lost out on a job because I didn't ask enough questions at the end, so I didn't seem interested enough in the role. The same thing happened to a friend who was a serial job interviewee, now she knows why! So, always prepare a few really good questions."

Charli, Videographer

Practise!

Borrow a friend to practise answering questions in a well-structured, confident manner.

VIDEO INTERVIEWS

Virtual interviews present a few extra challenges...

- Find somewhere quiet, clutter-free and away from distractions

- Check your tech

- Read all instructions (note timings and deadlines)

- Get familiar with the video chat platform

- Practise talking to a webcam

- And don't forget to smile, even if it's at a blank screen!

THE INTERVIEW

Destress | If you're feeling stressed before your interview, calm your nerves by focusing on breathing rhythmically: deep breath in, deep breath out. It will help you relax so you can be the best version of yourself. (See more mindfulness exercises in 'Take Care of You' on p.48.)

Wise words from a seasoned pro...

> Interviewers want you to be good; there's a lot of love in the room! They're not trying to catch you out. You've got to get your mindset into a place where you know they'd rather you did well; it's not adversarial. It's an opportunity for two people to talk about stuff.
>
> Just think: I'm good at some things, not good at other things, I've got lots of potential and I'd love to come and work for you. And if that doesn't happen, that's OK. Just be yourself, don't make things up. Try to talk from the heart. My job as an interviewer is to let an individual be as good as they can possibly be.

Chris, HR Professional

First impressions really count

Some studies suggest interviewers make up their minds in the first five minutes, then spend the rest of the interview looking for things to justify their decision. What is certain, is that the way you look, your body language and how you first speak, all instantly give the interviewer a gut feeling about you. So, this is your opportunity to ooze energy and enthusiasm!

- **Dress appropriately** for the company culture, whether it's face-to-face or a video interview. If in doubt, err on the smart side.

- Be **punctual** – ideally, 5–10 minutes early.

- Be **professional and courteous** to everyone you meet, from the receptionist to your interviewers. Make sure people remember you for all the right reasons!

- **Think confident body language:** smile and make eye contact with the interviewer. Give a firm handshake. Sit with good posture, be attentive and speak clearly.

- Start with a **positive** comment e.g. thank them for their time, say that you have been looking forward to the meeting, and why.

Be yourself

As a new graduate, employers won't expect the finished article, but they will appreciate a professional, decent person, who would fit in well with their company and help them grow the business: someone who is genuine, and shows enthusiasm, a good understanding of the role and a positive attitude – these things can go a long way.

Most importantly, be yourself. Do be truthful, and don't be afraid to express your informed opinions and ideas. But avoid any negative talk about employers, managers, tutors etc. as it looks unprofessional.

66 **It would be pretty remarkable if a new graduate had all the requirements for a job spec. Don't lie or exaggerate, turn it around and make a virtue of it: 'I don't have experience in X and Y, but I really want to learn about that and feel passionate about acquiring those experiences.' Honesty is very endearing in interviews.** 99

Jon, British Diplomat

If you're passionate about a cause – perhaps you've organised marches or demonstrations, or lobbied your local MP, or you write a blog with a strong following – you can bring this up if asked for examples of transferable skills like communication, organisation and commitment. But tread carefully.

Employment lawyer and diversity and inclusion expert Charlene Brown says: "You will spend a lot of time at the company you choose to work for. You have to be able to be yourself as much as possible even if some experiences may make you feel like you need to conform to the masses to be accepted or 'fit in'. It is important to be honest during an interview, especially if what you want to share is aligned with your values and what matters to you most.

"With that being said, it is important that you remember that not everyone may share your views or level of activism and not all activism is peaceful and legal. I say this to make sure that you treat others with professional respect that don't share your views and you demonstrate in your interview your ability to do so objectively and that your activism doesn't break any laws, rules or regulations that might be relevant to the company and industry you are thinking of working in."

"Talk about causes close to your heart if it makes you more interesting to the company you're trying to appeal to. And do it in a positive way by focusing on what you like, not what you hate e.g. You're passionate about preserving the planet, rather than you can't tolerate people who don't recycle. Use these passions and causes to show the transferable skills you have acquired."

Chris, HR Professional

50/50 conversation

An interview is just a fact-finding conversation; the employer is looking to see if you will be a good fit for them and equally, it's a chance for you to decide if they're right for you.

Help the conversation flow by asking intelligent questions, listen to the answers, and try to come up with follow-up questions. Aim to build rapport and make sure the interviewer walks away knowing those three key selling points on how you could add value.

Dealing with strange, unexpected questions

You can generally expect one or two tough questions, but some interviewers will throw in a real curveball.

These are not just trick questions, they serve one or more purposes: to reveal more about your personality and whether you'd be a good fit for the company, to assess your reactions under pressure, how you deal with difficult situations and solve problems and/or how creative you are.

Here are two genuine examples:

"What three things would you take with you to a desert island?"

How might you respond? Consider what these candidates' answers say about their characters:
Candidate 1: "A fishing rod, a camping knife and drinking water"
Candidate 2: "My labradoodle, a thick book and a bottle of wine"

"If you were asked to unload a jumbo jet full of Jelly beans, what would you do?"

With questions like this, there's clearly no right answer, but the interviewer will be interested in your reasoning; so feel free to ask questions for clarification, and do articulate your thought process e.g. "Do the Jelly beans need to be fit for eating afterwards? If not, I might start by using the luggage chutes."

If you are asked a question that catches you off guard, know that how you respond is less important than the way you handle the situation. So, don't get flustered, take your time, and try to retain a sense of humour! Just answer from the heart. It might be the 'right' answer, it might not, but that's OK.

Real examples of curveball questions:

If you were a fruit, what would you be?

Pick two celebrities to be your parents.

On a scale of 1–10, how weird are you?

Would you rather know a lot about a little or a little about a lot?

What superpower would you most like to have?

How many cows are in Canada?

How do I rate as an interviewer?

How would you get an elephant in a fridge?

How does the internet work?

If Germans were the tallest people in the world, how would you prove it?

Think how you might respond to some of these, and what your answers might reveal about you!

End on a high

Thank the interviewer for their time and restate your interest in the position.

Don't forget to follow up promptly with a written thank you.

ASSESSMENT CENTRES

If you are applying for graduate jobs or schemes, you will likely be invited to assessment days, which are often the final hurdle of the recruitment process. They are designed to give the employer a well-rounded appraisal of candidates' competencies, their motivation, likely performance in the workplace and fit with the company.

You'll be asked, along with other candidates (virtually, or at an assessment centre), to take part in a range of tasks and activities to evaluate specific skills, such as planning, communication and creativity.

Typical group exercises include discussions, case studies, presentations, problem solving and role play and you're also likely to face individual tasks and interviews. Before you attend, try to find out what type of assessments the employer uses and get in some practice; you'll feel far more confident if you know what to expect.

Here are some helpful pointers from HR professionals who design and run assessment centres:

Always on show

What you need to remember about assessment centres (without freaking out) is that you're on show 100% of the time. And, because of that, you've got to demonstrate stuff – don't just think it, you have to do it! For example, how can you prove you have listening skills? Catch the speaker in the eye, nod, and reflect back what they have just said.

Even if the day involves informal breaks or 'social activities', be aware that people can't help forming opinions about you!

TIP

IF YOU ARE OFFERED A CHOICE OF ASSESSMENT DAYS, OPT FOR THE EARLIEST DATE YOU CAN POSSIBLY ATTEND, TO AVOID ENDING UP ON A WAITING LIST OR MISSING OUT COMPLETELY. IF THE EARLIER ASSESSMENT CENTRES PRODUCE A GLUT OF STRONG CANDIDATES, COMPANIES WILL OFTEN CANCEL THE REMAINING DATES.

Find out what to expect

What you do and how you do it

With group exercises, often there's no right or wrong answer. Assessors are more interested in how candidates interact and reach a solution. They will observe what you say and how you say it. They'll look at your body language and how you engage with other people: are you positive and friendly, or confrontational? Do you remain calm? Are your notes well-organised or a bit of a mess?

Nobody is brilliant at everything so, remember, if one activity doesn't go so well, you will always have the chance to shine in another.

Don't get fixated on leadership

Be sure to contribute, but don't feel you need to dominate the tasks. There are all sorts of ways to show leadership qualities, for example:

- Bring people into the conversation: if you don't know much about the discussion topic, admit it and invite people to explain, ask questions, or check 'have we heard from everybody?'

- Take the role of organiser: 'We've got 45 minutes so let's clarify what we need to do on this task.'

- Own the flip chart: Offer to note down the main ideas so everyone can keep track.

* Bear in mind that, at graduate level, employers are more likely to be looking for good team players than strong leaders.

Relax and be yourself

Remember, you have been invited to the assessment day because the employer thinks you're good – they want to like you! So don't feel intimidated by other candidates. Just get into it and enjoy it.

show you are a team player

Get into it and enjoy it!

133

FOLLOW UP

It may seem obvious, but you should always follow up an interview or assessment centre with a thank you email or letter. In fact, this simple action might make all the difference. Whilst only a quarter of hiring managers actually receive a written thank you, 80% acknowledge it does help when reviewing a candidate, according to a survey by Accountemps. So, for a small amount of effort, you can really stand out!

As well as demonstrating courtesy, it's a chance to restate your interest and why you'd be a great employee. Thank the interviewer for the opportunity and try to personalise your note by referring to a highlight from your conversation. Send it promptly (within 24 hours), but don't stress too much about what to write, because the gesture itself is what people will remember.

If you are asked to follow up with a reference, portfolio or anything else, be sure to do so promptly (and always check your junk email folder so you don't miss anything important).

UNSUCCESSFUL THIS TIME?

Rejection is an inevitable and unavoidable part of job hunting. It happens to everyone, no matter how talented or skilled you are. While it never gets easier to miss out on a job you had set your hopes on, it's important to **focus on your strengths** and just **get your job hunt back on track.**

> "Rejections can feel soul-destroying but be resilient. Often, it's not you or how you performed, they were just looking for something else."
>
> Chris, HR Professional

If you're unsuccessful after an interview or an assessment day, **try to get feedback**. It could help with future applications and you might even be reconsidered (we have known candidates to be asked back for an interview and then be accepted).

And if you're not getting interviews, ask someone to check your CV and cover letter.

Just keep going – persistence pays off!

GOT THE JOB?

Congratulations, a job offer is fantastic!

In some situations, saying yes will be a no brainer – you'll know this is the job you want, no question.

But in others, you may want to take a little time to think over the offer, particularly if you're waiting to hear about a job you like better. Don't feel under pressure to say yes or no straight away.

It is courteous to send the employer a short email to thank them for their offer, reaffirm your interest and ask for some time to consider it, and when they need your decision. Don't hang on too long before sending an initial response, or the employer may think you're not interested and offer the job to someone else.

Think about the following points, to help you decide whether or not to accept, negotiate, or raise any questions with the employer:

- Take into account the whole compensation package, not just the salary. Other benefits can add a lot of value e.g. company car, private healthcare, performance-related bonus, pension, holiday entitlement.

- Consider the role, prospects, company culture, working hours, location and commute. Make sure it feels right and trust your instincts.

What are your options?

Accept the offer: Write a polite acceptance email confirming the details of the offer (including job title, salary, benefits and start date).

Negotiate: If you are interested in the position but feel the offer could be stronger, you could try negotiating. Have a clear picture of competitive salaries for the job and think about what package would work for you, then request a meeting face-to-face or on the phone. Bear in mind if you push too hard, the employer may withdraw the offer.

Decline: If you decide the position is not right for you, write a brief, polite email to decline the offer. It's important to maintain a positive relationship in case you ever want to apply to the company in the future.

Jot down three things you've learnt
so far that have surprised you...

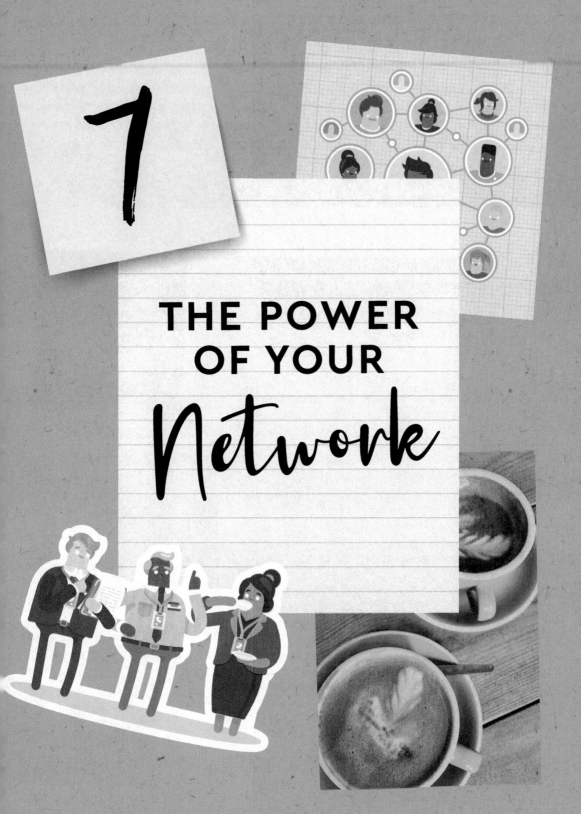

7

THE POWER OF YOUR *Network*

Networking is all about building relationships and getting to know people who can help as you figure out what career you'd like to do. This chapter explains why networking is so important for the world of work, why it needn't be remotely intimidating, and how you can help others who've helped you. There's a step-by-step guide to get you started, including how to get the most out of LinkedIn.

> 66 YOUNG PEOPLE DON'T REALISE THEY ALREADY HAVE LOADS OF CONTACTS. IT'S EVERYONE THEY'VE EVER MET: THEIR TEACHERS, PARENTS' FRIENDS. LEVERAGE THE HELL OUT OF THAT! 99
>
> CHRIS, HR PROFESSIONAL

Summer BBQ time!

Most of us find the thought of professional networking more than a little daunting. But actually, we're all <u>networking, all the time</u>, and helping others to do the same, without even knowing we're doing it.

Every time we have a conversation with someone we know, or a mutual friend introduces us to someone new, we're building relationships and nurturing our existing networks. And, throughout our lifetimes, these networks slowly expand.

Football

When you went off to university, your world suddenly got bigger than your family, your hometown, and your school friends. You made lifelong friendships, met inspiring tutors, took a bar job and got to know even more people. You joined a sports team, wrote articles for the student paper, or acted in plays and found others with shared <u>interests and passions</u>.

Flat 108 freshers 2022

It's after graduation – when you're taking your first tentative steps in the 'real' world and transitioning from education into the workplace – that the networks you've grown and nurtured over the years start to become helpful in another way.

Why
Networking Matters

Figures vary but studies show that anywhere between 70% and 85% of job vacancies may be found and filled through networking, rather than by companies advertising and recruiting for these roles.

Just as importantly, our networks can help us explore the industries and jobs we think we're interested in, and figure out exactly what it is we want to do.

Almost all graduates leave university with a fairly limited view of the world of work. A few weeks of industry experience may be the only insight you have. And that's no bad thing – we all have to start somewhere. But now is your chance to dig deeper, and discover more about the jobs and industries that most appeal. You can do this by asking the right questions to the right people.

It's not easy to 'wow' anyone with your CV when you're fresh out of uni. You're far more likely to win them over once they meet you, and see that you're smart, ambitious, engaging and more. That's another reason networking is worth the effort.

worth the effort!

* We're going to show you how to use your network to discover which career path is likely to be the most fulfilling and meaningful for you.

If you feel your career path is already mapped out, this chapter is still for you, because networking can create relationships that will be useful throughout your entire career (not just when looking for your first job).

> 66 *People make the best decisions when they have the best information.* 99
>
> *Jon, British Diplomat*

How to approach networking

Think of networking, first and foremost, as a series of <u>conversations</u> that allow you to learn about people, professions and industries.

Take it slowly, <u>develop trust,</u> and work just as hard on building existing relationships with those who can introduce you to people, as forging new ones.

You'll quickly find that most people are super happy to help. If advice is offered, <u>listen hard,</u> because it might just be useful in an interview one day.

"Start by fact finding, ask questions, find out what's out there. Don't be afraid to ask for help, it's a strength not a weakness. Most people are very willing to help, it makes them feel good. The worst thing that can happen is they say no. Then move on to the next person, don't be put off."

Mark, Career Coach

TIP

Before you start networking, you'll need a word-perfect CV, and a completed LinkedIn profile. There's lots on that in other chapters, so make sure you've followed those steps before you start connecting with people in industry.

A STEP-BY-STEP GUIDE

1. Identify your network

Start by mapping out your network on a big sheet of paper. You're in the middle, now add your immediate family and close relatives, jot down the names of your friends, and family friends, the people you've worked with, and then work outwards, like this:

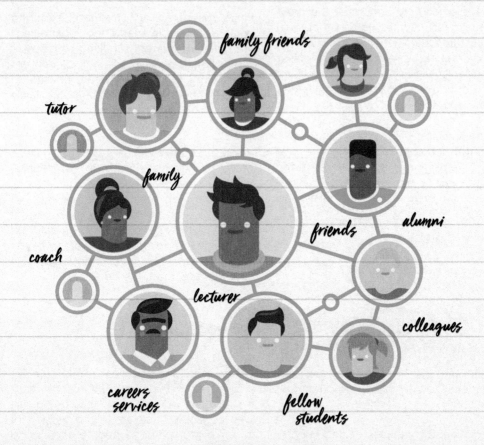

Think about all the people who have helped you get where you are today, be it your mum's best friend, your second cousin, a friend of a friend, an inspiring teacher, your five-a-side coach, or your Saturday job boss. All those people who have championed, mentored and encouraged you in some way form your existing network.

Even if none of these people work in the industry you want to work in, all of them have their own networks, some of whom will be relevant to you and your career goals.

2. Write your elevator pitch

What's an elevator pitch? A SHORT, SUCCINCT SUMMARY THAT CAN BE DELIVERED IN THE SAME TIME IT TAKES TO RIDE AN ELEVATOR!

Being equipped with a little spiel you can use when meeting or contacting new people will help you make the most of every opportunity, as you'll be able to communicate clearly what you're trying to do – whether that's learning more about working for small businesses and fledgling startups or figuring out what creative jobs there are in the technology industry.

A strong elevator pitch should cover, in a few tight sentences, <u>who you are and what you're hoping to do.</u> If there's time, you can add some information about your relevant experience, attributes and qualities.

A good opener might look like this...

> I'm a recent history graduate exploring what a career in marketing looks like. I am really interested in talking to industry professionals who work in B2C content marketing for established, household name brands who could help me learn more about what they do day-to-day.

Also, think about your '<u>so what</u>' factor. You're a graduate with a 2:1 degree. So what? What sets you apart from all the other job-seeking graduates, and makes you special? Do you have several weeks' work experience in three different companies under your belt, or have you won an award? That level of detail will give your elevator pitch the edge!

3. Make contact with your network

Your elevator pitch is memorised and you've identified everyone in your network. Great work!

Next, it's time to start approaching people. If you need to build confidence, begin by networking with people you know: you'll quickly get better at asking the right questions once you have had some practice. You'll find that people in your immediate network will try to put you in touch with their own contacts who they feel might be able to help.

Try to overcome your fear of phone calls, as picking up the phone can be far more fruitful than emailing or messaging (as well as faster). Use an edited version of your elevator pitch so people understand that your intention is to expand your professional network, and so they know which industries and careers you're most interested in.

Remember, if a friend or relative takes the time to introduce you to someone they know, always be proactive and follow up swiftly to set up a coffee meeting or a phone call.

4. Prepare well

All your networking has paid off and you've landed your first coffee meeting. The golden rule here is to prepare, prepare, prepare. Use LinkedIn and Google to do some thorough research on the person and their company in advance, write a list of questions and rehearse your elevator pitch. If you're a creative, bring your portfolio, or make sure it's ready to share digitally.

On the day itself, think about your presentation as first impressions count. Part of that is what you're wearing. If you're meeting someone in their workplace, you can ask about the dress code before you go. And, if in any doubt, dress on the smart side. Generally, if you look good, you feel more confident. But you also need to be comfortable as much as professional and appropriate. Don't be afraid to express your personality a bit through your wardrobe, if that's what feels comfortable.

When you first meet, give them a firm handshake, make eye contact, say their name and smile.

And remember, this isn't a job interview, it's an opportunity to find out more (you're the one asking the questions!). A good way to close the meeting is by asking if there's anyone else they think you should speak to.

Taking a few notes is fine, but don't let it affect your rapport or the impression you're seeking to make. We've created a handy worksheet you can fill in immediately afterwards.

When it's over, reflect on what you've learnt and take any actions, such as connecting with the person they suggested you meet, reading that article they recommended or looking up the company that might be hiring.

And always send an email within 24 hours to thank them for their time and for sharing their knowledge.

First impressions count!

143

5. Try a networking event or careers fair

Networking events can be scary, even for experienced folk: a room full of people you're supposed to be talking to, all deep in conversation. It's enough to make anyone's palms sweat. But, if you can conquer the terror, you'll find it's also a thrill. And the more you do it, the easier it gets.

> **Courage starts with showing up & letting ourselves be seen.**
>
> *Brené Brown, Professor, Lecturer & Author*

Event organisers will often send round a list of who's coming a day or two prior. That's your chance to <u>research</u> who you want to speak to and to <u>prepare</u> some intelligent questions for them. But it's also wise to have a few questions up your sleeve for anyone else you meet on the day too.

> **You walk into one of these events and everyone is in their circles talking. But most people are really welcoming, and you can do the same for others: make eye contact, smile and bring them into the conversation when they approach. Tell them what you were just talking about and ask what they do.**
>
> **Michael, Innovation Consultant**

TIP

If you can reference industry news in your conversation, you'll seriously impress.

Research & prepare

* As well as your elevator pitch, think of a couple of interesting stories to tell about yourself – perhaps about your latest work experience placement, or the charity fundraiser you led at university or the volunteer work you do. This will help you make a lasting impression.

Don't be afraid to break the ice, walk up to people and start talking – everyone is there for the same reason. It's much easier to strike up a conversation with someone who's standing on their own looking bored or lonely so make a beeline for them.

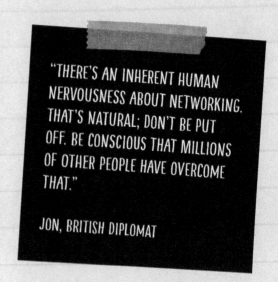

"THERE'S AN INHERENT HUMAN NERVOUSNESS ABOUT NETWORKING. THAT'S NATURAL; DON'T BE PUT OFF. BE CONSCIOUS THAT MILLIONS OF OTHER PEOPLE HAVE OVERCOME THAT."

JON, BRITISH DIPLOMAT

Kalkidan, Sancho's

Kalkidan, Co-Founder of Sancho's sustainable fashion, who set up her business as a new graduate...

" I wish I'd clocked on to the value of networking earlier. You can be clinical about it, or just be comfortable in your own skin and be drawn to people you'd like to know more about, and who want to know more about you, and just see what develops. Having our shop has meant we've met a whole range of people and we're starting to grow a good network within the industry. I'm excited to see what comes out of it. "

6. Seize every opportunity

Sometimes you can be networking without even knowing it. Perhaps you meet someone at a party who does the job you want to do. Be sensitive to the situation because no one likes to talk shop at a social gathering. Instead, ask them if you could contact them the next day to ask them some in-depth questions.

These 'organic' opportunities can also be manufactured. For example, instead of managing your job hunt from home, why not pop into a free co-working cafe with your laptop? The people using these spaces are typically there because working from home is lonely and isolating. That means they may be happy to chat.

The power of networking

employees, employers and business owners show how organic conversations can lead to worthwhile opportunities

"I GOT MY FIRST REPORTER'S JOB AFTER MEETING A NATIONAL NEWSPAPER JOURNALIST AT A PARTY. I TOLD HER I WAS TRYING TO GET INTO JOURNALISM, AND SHE GAVE ME HER CARD AND TOLD ME TO CALL HER THE NEXT MORNING. NEXT THING I KNEW I WAS ON TWO WEEKS' WORK EXPERIENCE ON THE NEWS DESK AND SIX MONTHS LATER I MADE IT ONTO THE TRAINEE SCHEME."

EMILY, PR BUSINESS OWNER

"After graduation I must have filled in around 50 job applications, but didn't get far, and often had no response at all from the employers. I started to contact people on LinkedIn, just to find out more about their businesses, and my luck began to change. I suddenly had a number of job leads. Then a casual chat at a stag do led to an introduction, which eventually led to my current job! My advice to people in similar situations would be to try networking first. You never know what might come out of a friendly conversation!"

Michael, Insurance Client Management

"I was working for an NGO in Malawi, and overheard a conversation in a bar between two English guys discussing the amazing venture they had set up: Malawi's first agri-fruit processing business, including a farming 'university'. They were really trying to make a difference. I was fascinated and started chatting to them. By the end of the evening, I had a job offer, joined them and loved it!"

LOUISE, BUSINESS DEVELOPMENT MANAGER

"I was having lunch at a hotel in London. The waitress was very engaging with lots of energy and positivity. She said she had been a part time actress at home in Romania. Within an hour my colleague offered her a customer-facing job at Madame Tussauds in London where she became a star employee!"

Peter,
Leisure business
Chairman

"Charli was a last-minute stand in to help out at an event, when someone dropped out due to illness. After a quick briefing, she was hands-on from the moment she arrived. We loved her friendly approach, initiative and can-do attitude. As a result we employed her. As a small business, we were able to shape the role to accommodate her career aspirations."

Sophie, Founder of a student/graduate support platform

"I have always enjoyed getting to know people; I networked for 20 years without thinking of it as networking! It meant that when I set up my own thing, I had loads of people to talk to, and when you're small, you only need one of them to give you some work. I got lucky, a lady I'd met at a golf event asked me to do some recruiting and that's how I started. One conversation just might make a difference, it doesn't have to be through work. So I'd say go to meetings and events if you get the chance. You'll meet some people you like and some you don't, just swap cards or emails."

Chris, HR Consultant

How to use LinkedIn® to network

A LinkedIn profile is your publicly viewable online CV, so it needs to be polished. We've dedicated a whole section on how to do that (pp.112–115) so, here, we'll assume your profile is complete and we'll look at how you can use LinkedIn for networking.

Approaching strangers cold is probably the least effective way to network on social media. Start by building your LinkedIn connections using your existing connections. Upload your online address book from your email account and you'll have a good-sized professional network full of people you already know to start with.

TIP

You can also download all your LinkedIn contacts into a spreadsheet so you can categorise them into useful groups e.g. prospective employers, recruiters, references.

You should always take the time to customise your connection requests with a friendly note by clicking 'add message' and, if you think it might be necessary, include a reminder of where you met, or who you met through.

Customise with a friendly note

Next, think about groups and organisations that could help you form new connections. A great place to start is by checking if your university, college or school have alumni groups on LinkedIn – and many do. Alumni can be a good source of help, having been through the same experience themselves.

As we mentioned earlier, networking isn't all about what you can gain, but what you can do for others. Engage with other people's posts by liking what they've written or writing words of encouragement. Introduce people to one another, or share and comment on articles that may interest your network.

* engage
* introduce
* share
* comment

If you've spotted someone you'd like to learn more from – perhaps an industry leader, or a friend of a friend – there's no harm in sending a connection request with a polite message asking them if they'd consider a short phone call with you. It's helpful to <u>explain your intentions clearly</u> i.e. that you'd love the opportunity to get their insight on the industry. It's also useful to demonstrate that you know who exactly they are. Did you enjoy hearing them speak at an event? Were you inspired by watching their TEDTalk or listening to their podcast?

While you should never ask someone for a job, you can ask questions about how to break into their industry, and what they might look for when flicking through a pile of graduate CVs.

Finally, don't forget that LinkedIn is a rich source of company information, as well as a professional networking site. You can use it to <u>learn more</u> about the brands and organisations you'd like to work for by searching for their company pages. Read these before doing any phone calls and interviews as it'll give you a better sense of the company culture, and you can really impress by showing that you've done your homework!

Disclaimer: LinkedIn is the registered trademark of LinkedIn Corporation or its affiliates. The use of the LinkedIn trademark in connection with this product does not signify any affiliation with or endorsement by LinkedIn Corporation or its affiliates.

Use LinkedIn®
to research!

GOLDEN RULES OF NETWORKING

Do

✓ **some basic research before you show up:** who's attending and what questions will you ask? Preparation is not only courteous and shows your enthusiasm, but it'll also mean you get far more out of the conversations as you won't have to waste time going over the basics.

✓ **make your LinkedIn profile the best it can be, as it's your online CV.**

✓ **think about what you can offer your new contacts:** perhaps a useful connection, a link to a relevant article or TED Talk, or a skill.

✓ **network on your terms.** Put your safety first especially if you're talking to strangers online. If anyone is inappropriate, or you feel uncomfortable, block and unfollow. Only ever meet new contacts for coffee in a public place – and not at their office address.

Don't

✗ **ask your contacts for a job;** it won't get you very far. You can, however, ask questions like: "How do you think I can make myself more employable?" or "do you know of any companies in your industry that employ graduates?"

✗ **rely on jobs boards alone to find work:** studies suggest many companies find other ways to fill the positions, including through their own networks!

✗ **network online only,** as you'll make deeper connections and a lasting impression face to face

✗ **be afraid to get in touch** with someone the morning after meeting them; it's polite and shows enthusiasm

"THE FIRST TIME YOU START NETWORKING IT CAN FEEL QUITE INTIMIDATING, AS A NEW GRADUATE SPEAKING TO SOMEONE WITH A LOT OF EXPERIENCE, BUT IT GETS EASIER; YOU LEARN AND YOU BUILD CONFIDENCE AND THEN EVENTUALLY YOU DON'T EVEN THINK ABOUT IT. I WOULDN'T HAVE HAD ANY OF MY SUCCESSES IF I HADN'T KEPT TALKING TO PEOPLE, KEPT SAYING YES."

CHLOË, EARLY CAREERS COACH

NETWORKING WORKSHEET

Meeting Details

Who: Contact: 📱

When: ✉

Where:

Three questions I want to ask them:

1.

2.

3.

Outcomes

What I learned that I didn't already know

This surprised me the most

Brilliant advice they gave me

Contacts they suggested I follow up with

What I need to do next (follow ups, actions, research)

And don't forget to write a 'thank you' email...

ELEVATOR PITCH

Write your elevator pitch
(See the tips on p.142).

Who are you?
What are you hoping to do (specific goal/career interest)?
What's your 'so what' factor that makes you stand out?

8

WHY WORK EXPERIENCE

Pays

Whenever we ask recent grads, employers or recruiters for their top tip for new graduates, it is nearly always..."Get some work experience!" In this chapter, we'll explore why it's so worth it, where to find it, how to nail your applications and get the best from your placement.

WHY IS WORK EXPERIENCE IMPORTANT?

You might have been fully focused on your university studies up until now, but it's a wise move to get some industry experience before you start applying for jobs. There's no doubt it will give you a competitive edge, but gaining practical knowledge is just as much about finding your path. And you might even get paid for your work.

From structured internships to informal shadowing, any insights into industries that appeal to you will be helpful. We'll look at where to find opportunities later in this chapter (pp.162–163)

"Whilst a degree gives you qualifications and makes you employable, recruiters favour candidates who are work-ready. There's no substitute for getting out there, observing how business is conducted, working as part of a team, even simple stuff like finding out whether or not you enjoy an office environment."

Patrick, Mentor & Business Adviser

CAREER DIRECTION
FIND OUT WHAT YOU DO AND DON'T LIKE

With just a few weeks of work experience under your belt, you'll have the chance to explore industries beyond the limitations of a Google search, discover roles you never knew existed, and figure out what sort of working environment gives you the thrills and what sucks at your soul.

It's a worthwhile exercise even if you are unsure what you want to do, as you can test the water without a long-term commitment.

"If you have left uni and find yourself in that scary state of limbo where you don't know what you want to do with your life, join the club. Some people have a good idea, but most don't.

So, decide what you might enjoy or be good at, what you'd like to learn, skills you want to develop; then go do it in a variety of places: different organisations, try internships, volunteer, go abroad. Take some time to try out things before you make a final decision on what to pursue. Stretch yourself! In the process, you'll acquire valuable transferable skills, which you can use in other jobs. And it will help you understand what you enjoy doing and where you can add value in the working world."

Peter, Business Consultant

Not only will work experience help guide your career choice, but understanding what a job entails will significantly improve your confidence for applications and starting full-time work.

> "EVEN IF YOU THINK YOU KNOW WHAT YOU WANT TO DO, A JOB MIGHT TURN OUT TO BE VERY DIFFERENT FROM WHAT YOU HAD IMAGINED. SO, MY RECOMMENDATION TO ANY GRADUATE IS TO SPEAK TO PEOPLE IN THAT LINE OF WORK TO UNDERSTAND THE REALITY OF THE DAY TO DAY. GET SOME EXPERIENCE TO SEE WHAT YOU LIKE OR DON'T LIKE ABOUT THE JOB."
>
> MONICA, BUSINESS ADVISER

155

BOOST YOUR EMPLOYABILITY

Your work experience could land you a graduate job but at the very least, it will give you a competitive advantage.

How employers see it

Just as placements give you a chance to try out different roles, they provide companies with an opportunity to test and vet young talent. It's well known that most employers consider their pool of interns first when hiring for entry-level positions.

So, for many leading employers, internship programmes are also selection processes: it's one of the main ways they recruit graduates. Get on the programme, impress your managers and, later, you could be offered a permanent position.

Smaller companies also use work experience schemes to vet candidates. They may not have the budget for big graduate recruitment drives (so you won't have seen them on campus at university careers fairs), but many will be open to hosting you for work experience if you approach them directly. And, even if there is no job vacancy to offer you, perform well and you'll be front of mind when an opening does appear.

We look at how to prepare an effective application later in this chapter ('Prepare Well' p.161).

When you first start job hunting, you'll notice most entry-level job adverts specify "experience" wanted (a word that makes anyone straight out of education panic!).

> " I DIDN'T EXPECT MUCH FROM MY WEEK'S WORK EXPERIENCE BUT, WITH SOME WISE WORDS FROM THE MOTHER HEN TELLING ME TO MAKE SURE I WAS PROACTIVE, HELPFUL AND THAT I DIDN'T LEAVE THE OFFICE PRECISELY WHEN THE CLOCK STRUCK 5PM – BECAUSE IT'S ALL ABOUT LEAVING AN IMPRESSION – IT ALL WORKED OUT RATHER WELL. GUESS WHERE I'M WORKING NOW?! MY ADVICE: EVEN IF IT'S JUST A WEEK, GET SOME WORK EXPERIENCE IN YOU! "
>
> GEORGIE, GEOGRAPHY GRADUATE FROM MANCHESTER UNIVERSITY, NOW WORKS IN MARKETING

While no employer expects a graduate fresh out of university to have an expansive CV or to be anywhere close to the finished article, they will want to see your potential, and this is where some industry-specific work experience can be invaluable.

Why? Mainly because it reduces the employer's risk: if they can see you've worked (however briefly) in their industry, it tells them you are committed, "work-ready" and importantly, you understand what you're walking into – therefore you're more likely to be satisfied and stick around (and good workers can be incredibly expensive to replace).

Time spent in a professional environment will equip you with industry knowledge and build transferable skills such as commercial awareness and teamwork. For your CV, applications and interviews, you will have specific examples to demonstrate your skills and attributes e.g. how you contributed to a project or helped resolve a client's problem.

For these reasons, relevant work experience is a key differentiator when comparing graduates with similar qualifications.

Build transferable skills

Get to know the people you work with

Opportunities for career advice & references

EXPAND YOUR NETWORK

Build your professional network by getting to know the people you work with and note down their contact details; they could help with career advice, provide references and possibly open up other opportunities in the future.

"Talking to colleagues, understanding what they do every day, how they got into the industry and then just getting to know them – that's what really brought it to life and convinced me I'd like to work in this field."

Henry, intern at an investment firm

EARN WHILE YOU LEARN

While some work experience – like shadowing people and volunteering for charities – is unpaid, other opportunities let you earn while you learn. And if you've graduated with an overdraft, this may be the time to look at these options a bit more closely.

Due to the value employers place on work experience, there has been a sharp rise in the number of companies offering paid schemes.

Despite disruption from the pandemic, over half the UK's leading employers expect to offer in-person work placements for students and recent graduates, with a quarter preparing to deliver training online. This includes course placements, vacation internships and an increasing number of companies also provide paid training programmes for 1st and 2nd year students, knowing that many of these successful placements lead to the recruitment of candidates for their graduate schemes.

Highfliers – The Graduate Market

So what are the rules around pay?

The majority of internships must now be paid at least the minimum wage, but there are some grey areas and exceptions e.g. working for charities or students doing an internship as part of their university course.

While there is currently no legal definition of an 'intern' under minimum wage law, your rights depend on your employment status:

Worker
Typically, if a company asks an intern to work set hours, perform set tasks, meet deadlines, perform the work of paid members of staff, work unsupervised or even manage other members of staff then, by law, they are considered a 'worker' and are entitled to be paid at least the minimum wage, whatever the length of the internship or placement.

Shadowing
However, if they are only 'shadowing' – that means observing employees who already work for the company to get a better understanding of their role – the company is not obliged to pay and they are not required to complete any tasks.

know your status

While most companies view internships and work experience placements as a chance to identify, nurture and attract talent, some exploit interns by using them as free labour. It's estimated that around a third of internships may be unpaid. Catching unscrupulous companies out unfortunately relies entirely on interns reporting the employer, which many are reluctant to do as they care about getting job references and future work opportunities. That's why it's important to understand your employment terms (including payment) **before** you sign up. It may also be possible to negotiate minimum wage.

If you can prove you were a 'worker' but were paid less than the minimum wage, it may be possible to claim 'back pay' for an internship via HMRC, even if you had agreed to work unpaid at the time. Check out Employment Rights & Pay For Interns on GOV.UK.

PLANNING YOUR PLACEMENTS – THINGS TO CONSIDER

BRAND AMBASSADORSHIPS

WORK PLACEMENTS

INTERNSHIPS

VOLUNTEERING

SHADOWING

FREELANCING

CONTRACT WORK

VIRTUAL INTERNSHIPS

PART-TIME JOBS

WORKING ABROAD

TEMPING

EMPLOYER OPEN DAYS

There are plenty of ways to explore careers and start building valuable business skills, from paid internships to volunteering. But before you leap in, have a proper plan so you choose wisely, secure the placements you want and reap rewards from your efforts.

How to choose

Having a clear strategy will make it easier to research companies, help you to write a more convincing application and get the most from your experience in a workplace.

Think about:

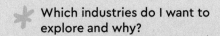 Which industries do I want to explore and why?

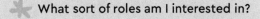 What sort of roles am I interested in?

* What type of work do I want to try?

* What topics/projects did I enjoy at uni, that I would like to look into further?

* What skills am I hoping to develop?

* What sort of culture might suit me?

* What would I like to have achieved by the end of my placement?

What type of organisation?

Ideally, spend time in big and small businesses – they offer different but equally valuable experience:

Large, high-profile companies might give you formal training on bigger projects.

In smaller companies, the training may be less structured but more hands-on. You could benefit from greater responsibility and exposure to more areas of the business, all of which would make you an attractive proposition for a larger employer, if that was your ultimate goal.

Non-profits and charities offer volunteering opportunities as well as work experience. Be aware that volunteering is unpaid, but it is highly valued by employers, because it demonstrates social conscience as well as worthwhile skills such as teamwork, resourcefulness and self-motivation.

Prepare well

Apply early

Ideally, start looking well before you want to do a placement, because some involve a lengthy selection process, and you may need to send a lot of applications to receive only a few replies. Bear in mind top company schemes get booked up fast, so it's wise to apply early.

Before making any approaches, be sure to have everything ready.

Create a hit list

Take the time to research different organisations to check they could provide the type of experience you need, and to help you customise your application. Don't be tempted to fire off loads of vague, generic applications; employers want to know why you're keen to get experience in their organisation specifically, so a one-size-fits-all approach simply won't work.

If you can't find any details on how to apply for work experience, there's no harm in calling the company's reception, and asking for contact details. Normally, you'll just be given a name and email address, but be prepared to impress on the phone just in case.

Prepare your CV & cover email

If the company you're approaching has a work experience application process, be sure to complete every step carefully. However, most companies will simply ask you to submit a covering email with an attached CV. So, show you've done your research, let them know why you're interested and well-suited to their company. Tailor your CV to highlight your most relevant skills and attributes. It might be time-consuming but putting in the effort means you're much more likely to be successful.

TIP:
Try to find out who oversees work experience placements; submit your application to them and address them by name in your cover email – it will create a good impression and has far more chance of being read!

Sort out your digital footprint

It's sensible to assume that employers will check your social media profiles before taking you on, so make use of privacy settings to ensure everything that is publicly viewable is appropriate for them to see!

See more tips on all aspects of applications including cover letters, CVs and online profiles in 'Job Hunting: How to Stand Out' (pp.103–136).

WHERE TO FIND WORK EXPERIENCE OPPORTUNITIES

Networking

Networking can be a great way to find work experience opportunities. Start with people you know – parents, friends, relatives etc. and see 'The Power of Your Network' chapter on how to explore further afield. Find out if anyone has suitable contacts in the industry, ask if you could come in for a few days' shadowing or if they offer placements you could apply for. Also go along to networking events or careers fairs.

Uni careers service

Your university careers centre will help even after you've graduated.

Alumni networks

Find these on LinkedIn and Facebook and connect with your fellow grads.

Your university tutors

Many will be working in industry or doing research, and are likely to have useful contacts, so see if they can help.

Jobs boards

Some organisations advertise their placements on jobs sites.

Company websites & socials

Check the jobs and blogs sections on company sites and social media, for advertised work experience schemes.

Speculative approaches

You don't have to wait for placements to be advertised, you can approach companies you want to work for directly by phone and email. It shows enthusiasm and initiative, which is always a good start. Find out how to do a speculative application on p.125.

> **"** AS NONE OF THE COMPANIES I WAS INTERESTED IN WERE ADVERTISING INTERNSHIPS, I DECIDED TO FIND CONTACT INFO FOR THE COMPANY OWNERS AND DIRECTORS AND EMAIL THEM DIRECTLY. I SENT A COVER LETTER AND MY CV. PERSISTENCE PAYS OFF IN THE END... I PROMISE! **"**
>
> ABBI, GRADUATE IN ENGLISH, NOW ENJOYING A PR INTERNSHIP

LinkedIn company pages

Follow companies you like as many post internships and job opportunities. Get onto their radars by liking and/or commenting on their posts and joining relevant groups, where you'll meet like-minded people. See 'Job Hunting: How to Stand Out' (pp.112–115) for how to get the most out of LinkedIn.

Freelancing

For many fields (e.g. creatives, digital, languages, accounting, social media, tutoring), freelancing is a relatively quick way to accumulate experience, prove your skills and expand your network, as well as giving you an insight into what types of organisations suit you best. Better still, the flexible hours mean you can fit work around job hunting or studying.

Temping

Paid temp work will give you an insight into industry, a chance to learn new skills, and access to professionals across different fields. You can find temporary positions on jobs boards, company websites, through speculative approaches, and by signing up with temp agencies. Just bear in mind that employers must pay agencies a cut for every hour you work, so you may find you earn a higher rate by applying directly.

Venture abroad

How about combining travel with work experience? Time abroad will undoubtedly increase your confidence, develop cultural awareness and build transferable skills such as communication, organisation and self-motivation.

Go it alone or check out some of the many organisations who run internships or volunteering abroad programmes. But before you hop on the next flight, do proper research to make sure it's a reputable company with good reviews, and try to get in contact with other grads who've trodden the same path.

Virtual internships

A fairly new concept, but they have some seriously good benefits for both interns and businesses. Interns don't have to cover travel costs, or relocate in order to get work experience, and businesses can cast their nets wider to find the best talent. Provided the company offering the internship has invested in video and communication apps and has a track record of supporting remote workers, they can be really good. Virtual interns should ideally be assigned mentors to set work and monitor their progress, and buddied up with employees who can offer encouragement and insights.

WHAT'S NEXT?

No reply?

If you don't hear back from a company you've approached, it's sensible to follow up and check your email hasn't been missed or lost. A polite phone call is usually the most effective way to get a quick response – and it shows an employer that you're confident, proactive and a strong communicator.

If you're not getting any offers, don't give up, but do reassess your approach. See how to make the best impression in 'Job Hunting: How to Stand Out' p.103.

Successful application?

Congratulations!

But before you accept, there are a few important things to check:

- Do find out what you'll be doing on your placement to ensure it will meet your objectives (you don't want to be *just* filing or photocopying for a whole month).

- Make sure you're clear about your employment terms including whether you will be paid. (As explained in 'Earn While You Learn' on p.159, by law, some types of placements mean you should be paid at least the minimum wage.) You'll need to know where you stand to determine if you can afford to cover any associated costs yourself.

- It's also worth asking if there's a chance of securing a permanent position at the end.

HOW TO GET THE MOST FROM WORK EXPERIENCE

Your work experience can be great preparation for the professional world – a chance to learn new skills, make useful contacts, get a taste of an industry and discover what you do or don't want to do. But it's down to you to get the best from the experience you've arranged. You'll need to approach it with enthusiasm and really get stuck in. Here's how to make sure you reap the maximum benefit from your time at work...

Do some (more!) research before you start

A little preparation can really pay off. A basic understanding of the business and the industry it operates in will enable you to engage in conversation with colleagues, ask sensible questions and generally create a positive impression early on. If you go in enthusiastic and informed, you are also less likely to find yourself burdened with menial tasks. You could also identify areas of work that particularly appeal, where you would like to get involved.

Make a good impression

You only get one chance to make a first impression! Turn up on time and dress suitably (if in doubt, opt for smart). Be friendly, introduce yourself to people. And relax, it's not all a huge test. So be yourself, always professional, but have some fun! Let them see that you're a great person to have around. Tune into your environment. If your co-workers are taking turns to make tea, make sure you offer too.

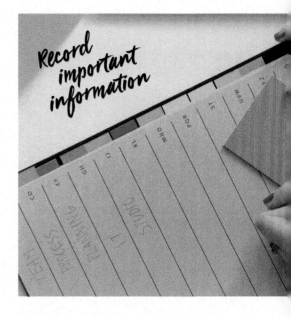

Record important information

Be organised

Listen carefully to instructions and note down important information like deadlines and meeting dates. Make sure you have all the information you need to carry out tasks and manage your time effectively.

Make sure you're on time!

164

Don't be afraid to ask questions

Be curious

You are there to learn and no-one will expect you to know everything. Don't be afraid to ask questions or seek clarification on anything you're unsure about; it will just show you are keen to do the job well.

Watch, listen and learn: you can glean a lot from the conversations going on around you (particularly useful if you're not getting as close to the action as you'd like). Rather than waiting around for the next task, ask if you can shadow someone or sit in on a meeting. Observing can give you a real insight into a role.

> "The most important learning curve for me was 'if you don't ask, you don't get.' I could have gained more from my work experience if I had pushed for them to involve me more."
>
> **Sophie, Marketing Intern**

Get to know people

Talk to your colleagues. Ask about their roles and how they got to where they are now – most people will be flattered that you are interested. You will learn plenty about the business and it's a golden opportunity to build connections that might prove fruitful later on (networking!). Take contact details and keep in touch after you have left e.g. by connecting on LinkedIn.

Be proactive

Whatever the task, however small, use your initiative to go above and beyond what is asked of you. Perform well and you are likely to be given greater responsibility.

If you have a constructive suggestion, don't be afraid to speak up – employers love people with opinions and ideas! Generally, try to get involved, offer to help out where you can.

"HOWEVER SMALL OR MUNDANE THE TASK YOU ARE GIVEN, DO AN ABSOLUTELY EXCELLENT JOB. DO IT BETTER THAN PEOPLE EXPECT. IF YOU'RE GIVEN A PROJECT, TAKE OWNERSHIP AND RESPONSIBILITY. A POSITIVE CAN-DO ATTITUDE WILL GET YOU NOTICED. IT'S UNLIKELY YOU'LL BE GIVEN TASKS BEYOND YOUR CAPABILITY, SO EMBRACE EVERY CHALLENGE AND GIVE IT YOUR BEST."

PETER, BUSINESS CONSULTANT

Take lots of notes!

Take notes

Keep a pen and notepad handy to jot down any useful information or advice.

Also, note the tasks you worked on, skills you developed, what you learned and achieved (ready for CV and job applications!). See our handy worksheet over the page.

Speak up and get involved!

"I made a list of everyone I met. In fact, I wrote a lot of notes... things people said I found interesting, pieces of advice, jargon or any snippets of information I felt I should remember. It was useful to look back on, especially when I was applying for jobs, to remember whom I had met, where I had been and what I enjoyed most."

Lotty, Intern at an Estate Agent, who went on to work in the property sector

Try to get feedback during the placement

Reflect

Once you have finished, take time to reflect on what you enjoyed and what you didn't, in terms of the work, company culture and the industry. For example, perhaps you loved the challenge of dealing with customers, but would feel more comfortable in a structured environment with clearer guidelines.

Even if you did not enjoy the placement at all, don't worry, that's what work experience is all about. You will have picked up skills and experience that will benefit any future career, and you'll have a clearer idea of what you **don't** want to do – and that's helpful too!

Ask for feedback

Try to get informal feedback from your supervisor during your placement, so you have the chance to improve where necessary. Nobody will expect you to be perfect from the outset, but they will be impressed if you show you can learn and adapt.

Follow up

Whether you have met someone for an informal chat, an interview, a day's shadowing or a month-long internship, always follow up with a written thank you (email or letter). Not only does it show good manners, it will help make sure people remember you. And don't forget to reaffirm your interest and enthusiasm for the company.

"Take from it what you can — you can take positive things out of even a bad situation, for example you met a great person, you learned how to do something (or how not to!). Always be learning and you'll never come out of an experience regretting it."

Mark, Career Coach

Take time to reflect

WORK EXPERIENCE WORKSHEET

Use this worksheet to keep consistent records of your work experience, so you have all the important information in one place, ready to update your CV, or for job applications and interviews. It will also help you reflect on how well the experience suited you, and what to look for next.

Date

Company

Contact details

Note what tasks you did, what you accomplished, what you learned, using this STAR method (explained fully in 'Job Hunting: How to Stand Out', p.122). It's an effective way to articulate skills and achievements. (Situation > Task > Action > Result).

Situation	Task	Action	Result

Comments/observations on the role, work environment, culture

Anything you realised will be really important to you

Any action to follow up (also note in your calendar)

Contact details of anyone who agreed to provide a reference:
name, position, email, phone, notes

Other contacts you made: name, position, email, phone, notes

Summing Up

Whether you do a work placement, a summer internship, freelance projects or volunteering, the skills and experience you accumulate will help decide your career direction, build confidence and improve your employability, provide useful contacts and could earn you some cash.

And it just might land you your first graduate job...

9

YOUR
MONEY
Matters

Money 101: In this chapter, we talk about how to manage your money, from bank accounts to budgeting, to setting spending and savings targets, because a little bit of planning now can go a long way towards preventing money problems later. We've included money-saving tips and a useful finance jargon buster. Read on for the lowdown on your student loan (and why it's not so scary), and dealing with debts. And, finally, we've recommended some reliable, unbiased sources for further info and financial support if you need it.

Manage my money?! What money, we hear you cry! After uni, there's an expectation that you'll start to become financially independent now you can be earning full time. But, the reality is there's likely to be a gap between graduation and a paid job that can support you fully, not to mention student debt looming like a rain cloud overhead.

In truth, adjusting to post-university life may mean managing on a fairly tight budget for many months. Whatever your situation, it's important to get to grips with your financial position – what you have, and what you owe – so you can take control and make informed decisions, with a clear understanding of any longer-term implications.

72% of people in their twenties make 'regrettable' money mistakes, with one in six admitting their debts 'spiralled out of control' in their first years of financial independence.

— MoneyHelper

The most important lesson of all is don't bury your head in the sand: ignoring issues like credit card debt will only make the situation worse.

26.35
12.54
+54.98
£ 93.87

FIRST STEPS

1. SWITCH TO A GRADUATE BANK ACCOUNT

First things first. Now you're no longer a student, it's time to open a graduate account, or a regular current account with the most favourable terms you can find. Some banks will move you to a graduate account automatically after you leave uni, but speak to your bank to double check this.

Despite the lack of juicy perks served with a student account, a graduate account is great for anyone with a large overdraft to pay off after university. Most banks cushion the blow by reducing the free overdraft limit annually, so you can gradually reduce your debt and pay back what you owe over two or three years. Standard current account overdrafts for everyone else are not so generous.

Even if you have an overdraft, you can still move to a graduate account with another bank. Shop around to find the best account available to you; there's no need to stay loyal if the terms are better elsewhere.

Look at important points like the bank's fee-free overdraft – is it £2,000 or £500 and how does it change over time? What financial penalties would you incur for things like going over your overdraft limit?

If you don't use your overdraft (lucky!) and you don't plan on needing to, you might want to pick a current account based on different criteria e.g. the best interest rate, or the best customer service.

One thing to note: most current accounts are available either as a standard, or a 'packaged' account, which offers extra features. In return for paying a monthly fee, you get benefits like car breakdown cover and insurance for travel and tech. But don't pay for extras you don't really need. If you don't have a car, breakdown cover is more or less useless, and your mobile phone may already be covered for theft and damage on your parents' home insurance policy (but double check).

What is an interest rate?

An interest rate is a percentage charged on the total amount you borrow or save. If you have savings, you'll earn the bank's specified interest rate. If you're in debt, you'll have to pay the lender's interest rate on what you owe. Not all interest rates are created equal: banks choose what interest rates they offer their customers, which is why you should shop around to find the best rates. (N.B. When talking about credit cards, we tend to use the term APR – Annual Percentage Rate – instead of interest).

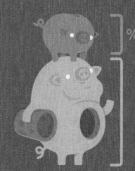

2. MAKE A BUDGET

You don't need to be good at maths to create a budget. You just need to know what money is coming in (e.g. salary or benefits) and what's going out (e.g. rent and living expenses) each month.

> ❝ ALTHOUGH 59% OF STUDENTS ATTEMPT TO BUDGET (EVEN IF THEY DON'T ALWAYS STICK TO IT), ONE IN 10 FIND THEMSELVES OVERSPENDING, 3% DON'T CONSIDER THEIR SPENDING AT ALL, AND 4% HAVE NO CONFIDENCE IN THEIR MONEY MANAGEMENT ABILITIES. ❞
>
> - NATWEST

A budget will help you to answer these important questions:

1. Are you living within your means?
Do you have spare cash, or are you spending more than you earn (eating into savings or running up debts)?

2. How much can you afford to spend?
How much money do you have left after paying for essentials e.g. rent, bills and food? What are your priorities? Where can you cut costs if necessary? Could you save any money?

You can use a budget planner tool or app to help record and analyse all your income and outgoings, or set up your own spreadsheet. If you'd rather do it by hand, use our budgeting table across the page.

to buy:
- ~~surfboard~~ flippers
- ~~vodka~~ juice
- ~~dog~~ goldfish
- ~~trainers~~ flip-flops
- ~~car~~ bike

BUDGETING PLANNER

	GOING IN		AMOUNT		
	Take-home wages from jobs (after tax, National Insurance, student loan and pension have been deducted)		£		
	Allowance from family if applicable		£		
	Side hustles (e.g. babysitting, dog walking, tutoring, copywriting, website design, social media, selling crafts)		£		
		TOTAL	£		
	COMING OUT				
	Rent		£		
	Bills		£		
	Subscriptions		£		
	Insurance		£		
	Clothes		£		
	Travel		£		
	Car (petrol, tax, MOT)		£		
	Socialising/hobbies		£		
	Gifts (Christmas / birthday)		£		
		TOTAL	£		

Do you have more going out than coming in? What spending could you cut?

10 IDEAS FOR FAST, EFFECTIVE WAYS TO SAVE OR MAKE MONEY

1. Switch! If you pay bills, or if you have a mobile phone, you may be paying over the odds, especially if you've been with the same provider for as long as you can remember. The thriftiest people switch providers every year, or as often as their contracts allow, so they are always getting the cheapest deals reserved for new customers, often with juicy perks thrown in. You might be able to get a better deal with your current provider by telling them you've found a cheaper quote elsewhere, which could save the hassle of switching.

2. Cancel subscriptions to things like Amazon Prime and Spotify (they're nice to have, but maybe your sister has a login you can use!).

3. Spread the bill for Christmas over months, not weeks. Start shopping for presents in the summer sales and store them until December.

4. Don't buy anything without checking for a deal or promo code online, and on social media, first. Often you'll need to sign up to a newsletter, but you can always unsubscribe as soon as you've got the code.

5. Shop for food at the right time of day. Half an hour before closing, some supermarkets put out heavily-discounted items so you can grab a bargain.

6. If you're working, make your own coffee in the morning and take a packed lunch. The savings added up over weeks are significant.

7. Don't buy new clothes, swap things you don't want with friends and scour charity shops for vintage finds that no one else will be wearing. (It's also eco-friendly!)

8. Sell whatever you no longer need. You can get decent amounts for selling old mobile phones and computers on tech recycling sites.

9. Monetise a skill: can you knit scarves, make jewellery, tile a bathroom, or draw pet portraits? Take some quality photos and make a portfolio on Instagram, or build a simple website, and start advertising what you can do on social media, and to friends and family.

10. Speak to your neighbours and find out if anyone needs any odd jobs done. The possibilities are just about endless: washing cars, hanging pictures, cleaning, gardening, dog walking. There are several websites and apps that connect local people who need tasks to be done, to those willing and able to help.

"When I first moved to London, my uni mates started a monthly beer and burger night. We take it in turns to organise and have a few pints and a bite to eat. It's inexpensive and we always have a really good night out, just catching up. Our house rule is you're not allowed to not attend unless you have a really good reason. There are lots of ways to live within your means and still have fun, you just have to keep track of what you're spending and understand that life's more expensive outside uni without student discounts and cheap drinks."

Adam, Investment Manager

"IF YOU'RE A KEEN CYCLIST THEN MAYBE YOU CAN SAVE YOURSELF THE COST OF THAT MONTHLY TRAVEL CARD (WHICH BY THE WAY IS A WHOPPING £150+ PER MONTH FOR ZONES 1-2 IN LONDON). THIS WILL HELP SAVE ON YOUR GYM MEMBERSHIP TOO - TWO BIRDS, ONE STONE. PLEASE WEAR A HELMET THOUGH!"

GRACE, TALENT AGENT

3. SET SPENDING & SAVINGS TARGETS

Squirreling away cash, however little, will give you more financial freedom and choice later on. Once you're earning and your financial situation allows, start by putting a portion of your take-home pay in an easy access account, which lets you withdraw money without any delay, or Premium Bonds, which can also be accessed quickly.

This becomes your pot for emergencies like car repairs, boiler breakdowns, or losing your job. Some money experts recommend aiming to save enough money to support yourself for three months without pay.

You can also start saving for specific goals, like a holiday, car, or a deposit for renting or (a much bigger deposit) for buying a home. If it's a long-term savings goal, look at savings accounts that pay a better rate of interest if you don't withdraw money for a fixed period.

It's a really good idea to set up a monthly standing order that drip-feeds money into a savings account because you're far more likely to save if you commit to putting away a regular sum at the beginning of the month, rather than waiting to see what's left at the end.

Bronwen got into the savings habit early on, when she first started earning from her paper round aged 13!

"At the start of the month, I pay all my outgoings and put a little away into savings, then I know what I have left for the month. At the moment I'm saving for the future, whether that's to start my own business, move abroad or buy a house. I know that I'm going to need it. Some people might say that you're not doing as much as you want now, but I think it seems silly to spend everything I've got and then find myself in a sticky situation where I can't afford my dream in the future."

**Bronwen,
Designer**

"A good guide is to allocate 50% of your monthly income to your core requirements (housing, utilities, council tax, food), 30% to discretionary (fun!) and 20% to saving. Automate the savings process and only spend what's left over."
Dennis Harhalakis, Founder of Cambridge Money Coaching

4. UNDERSTAND YOUR STUDENT LOAN

Many of you will be feeling pretty freaked out about the balance of your student loan but read this quick explanation of how the system works, and hopefully you will stop worrying.

Far more relevant than the amount of money you owe is the amount you actually repay, because your student loan is not a normal debt. It acts more like a graduate income tax that kicks in only once you start earning more than a specified threshold.

Unlike commercial loans (in which you must pay back the amount borrowed + interest), student loan repayments are calculated on how much you earn, not how much you owe. So, if you don't earn enough, you don't repay anything. And if your income drops, so do repayments.

If you're employed, your student loan repayments will be automatically deducted from your salary once you earn over the threshold. And if you're self-employed, HMRC will work out your repayments from your tax return.

The amount you borrowed does accrue interest during university and after graduation. But in the case of student loans, it's important to remember that what you are charged is not necessarily what you'll pay because, if you haven't repaid your loan within the time limit, which will be 30 or 40 years (depending on when you took out the loan), the debt is wiped. For many people, paying off a student loan early does not make good financial sense.

The psychological connotations of 'being in debt' are worse than the financial reality of a student loan, with many graduates feeling uncomfortable about owing large sums of money, and believing it may influence their choices on careers, living situations and other opportunities. But if you can get your head around the fact that your student loan is not real debt, you should start feeling better about it.

> "THE SYSTEM IS, IN REALITY, A GRADUATE CONTRIBUTION, DESIGNED SO THAT, IN THE MAIN, THOSE WHO GAIN THE MOST FINANCIALLY OUT OF UNIVERSITY CONTRIBUTE THE MOST."
>
> MARTIN LEWIS, MONEYSAVINGEXPERT

While your student loan doesn't work like debt (you'll pay it off through the tax system), **you do need to keep The Student Loans Company informed of any change of address or contact details.** If you don't, they may set higher penalty rates, also known as a 'non-compliance interest rate', for failing to respond to requests for information or for losing touch.

You can log in to your student loan repayment account on GOV.UK to update The Student Loans Company if your details have changed, to check the balance on your loan, or to make a lump sum repayment.

5. PRIORITISE PAYING OFF YOUR (OTHER) DEBTS

While you shouldn't rush to pay off your student loan, you do need to make paying off any other debts a priority before you start saving.

The higher the interest rate, the faster debt grows. So you'll need to focus on reducing your highest-interest debts first e.g. store cards, bank loans or student credit cards.

If you can't pay them off right away, you can normally lighten the load by switching loans to cheaper interest rate options. For example, if you've got credit card debts from uni and the lender is charging you lots of interest, you may be able to do a balance transfer to a credit card that charges 0% APR for a fixed period of time, meaning the balance will stay the same rather than getting worse each month, while you pay it off. But **always check lock-in clauses** to see if you would incur penalties by switching loan provider or paying off debts early.

For flexible borrowing like credit and store cards, the minimum payment indicates the lowest amount you must pay to avoid a charge. You will pay interest on the balance. But paying only the minimum takes longer to clear the debt, so you pay interest for longer and your total repayment will be higher. Pay off as much as you can afford each month, and ideally, clear your monthly balance as fast as you can to avoid paying any interest at all.

What's a credit score?

Your credit score determines how much of a risk you represent to lenders. Any form of credit including bank accounts, loans (except your student loan), retail store cards and mobile phone contracts all contribute to your credit history. There are lots of ways you can improve your credit rating, which will help you get better terms on things like mortgages later in life, but the basics include adding yourself to the electoral roll, avoiding late payments on bills or credit cards and not going over your overdraft limit.

It is basically the law that all recent graduates fall into one of two categories:

1. Sensible, level headed people who left university and walked straight into a nicely paying job that offers pay rises every year. Lives in nice rented flat in sensible area such as Battersea or Clapham. Will often say things like 'I just booked a skiing holiday – only 600 quid which I thought wasn't too bad right?', whilst you scream silently into your hands remembering how your card got declined earlier trying to buy a toe ring!

2. People who decided to pursue a career in the 'arts'. HAHAHAHAHA (manic laugh). Lives in silly area like Hackney, or Peckham in a tiny box or a freezing warehouse. Pays for everything with fingers crossed under the counter.

If there's a birthday dinner at that restaurant where the bread basket costs more than your monthly rent, simply take a deep breath and give birthday friend a ring BEFORE the event to explain that you'd love to come but you'll be having a starter and not splitting the bill, or you'd love to be there but you'll join for drinks after the meal. These are your friends and they'll understand. And if they don't...best get yourself some new mates!

Milly, Writer

BEWARE FINANCIAL SCAMS.

Never give out your bank account details unless you know exactly who you're dealing with (especially if they've called you). Banks won't request this information by email, nor will they ever ask for your PIN or your whole security number. Note that banks usually contact you by post or through your online banking messaging system, so always be suspicious of email. Also beware of emails that appear to be from HMRC. These phishing scams can look legitimate and sophisticated. If you get a payment or rebate notice you weren't expecting, always verify their authenticity by calling HMRC using the phone number on their website (not the number on the documentation you've received) before making a payment or giving out personal details.

GET HELP WITH FINANCIAL PROBLEMS

If you're struggling with your finances and you're facing escalating debts or have fallen behind with rent or bills, tackle the problem straight away so it doesn't get any worse:

Do

✓ Check if you're entitled to claim benefits (e.g. Universal Credit) to ease your situation; it's best to pursue any claim without delay, because it can take a while to process. Search gov.uk/benefits

✓ Talk to your bank, or seek free, confidential advice from a debt advice service:

National Debtline (0808 808 4000) or use their online service: My Money Steps

StepChange Debt Charity (0800 138 1111)

MoneyHelper (moneyhelper.org.uk)

Business Debtline, a national debtline service for the self-employed (0800 197 6026)

Don't

✗ Don't ignore debt problems. They will only get worse as interest and late payment charges build up, and they will also harm your credit rating, making future borrowing (including getting a mortgage one day) more difficult.

✗ Don't borrow more to pay off existing debt, because that can lead to money problems spiralling out of control.

UNDERSTANDING YOUR FIRST PAY SLIP

If you're an employee new to the world of work, getting your first pay slip can be a little confusing. There's the amount you were supposed to be paid, lots of unfair-looking deductions, and the amount that's actually going to be landing in your bank account.

The biggest amount is what's called your gross salary (before any deductions). What you're actually paid is called your net salary, also known as your 'take-home pay'. Those deductions could be:

Income tax: We all have to pay a proportion of our earnings to the taxman. Just make sure that you're on the right tax code so that you're being taxed correctly and not under or over paying. Call HMRC if you aren't sure.

National insurance: Another tax on earnings that goes into a fund from which some state benefits – like the state pension, statutory sick pay and maternity leave – are paid.

Student loan: Explained in more detail on p.179. You'll start repaying only once you begin earning over a certain threshold.

Pension contributions: If you earn more than a specified amount, your employer must set up and contribute into a pension for you. You will also be given the option to contribute to your pension, and you can choose how much. This is still your money, you just won't be able to spend it until you retire.

Cycle to work scheme: If you sign up to your employer's cycle scheme to get a tax-free bike, you will see monthly deductions taken from your salary.

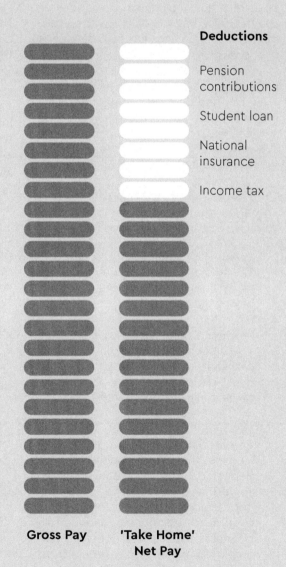

Deductions

Pension contributions

Student loan

National insurance

Income tax

Gross Pay

'Take Home' Net Pay

FINANCIAL JARGON

Tax year
This starts on 6 April and ends on 5 April the following year.

Gross income
This refers to your total earnings before taxes or other deductions. It includes all sources of income e.g. salary, wages, tips, rental income, savings interest, dividends or capital gains.

Income tax
A tax charged on most types of personal income. Taxes are used to fund public services (e.g. NHS, education, the welfare system) and infrastructure (e.g. roads, railways, housing).

Tax allowances and tax reliefs
These let you reduce the amount of tax you have to pay on income you receive.

> **Personal Allowance**
> The amount of income you're allowed to earn each year, before you start paying income tax.

> **Personal Savings Allowance (PSA)**
> The amount of tax-free interest you can earn each year on your savings (most people won't have to pay any tax on their savings interest).

> **Tax relief**
> Certain expenses are 'tax deductible' (i.e. the amount you spend can be deducted from your total earnings, so you have less income to pay tax on). E.g. you can claim for the cost of uniform, equipment, and certain business expenses if you're self-employed or if you're required to work from home.

Tax band and rate
This defines how much tax you pay on all earnings above your tax-free Personal Allowance. Most people pay tax at the basic rate.

HMRC
Her Majesty's Revenue & Customs is the Government department responsible for the collection of UK taxes.

National Insurance Contributions (NICs)
As well as income tax, you pay National Insurance on earnings above a specific threshold. Your contributions build your entitlement to certain benefits e.g. the state pension and maternity allowance.

National Insurance number
This unique number is used by HMRC to track your tax and National Insurance payments. It is normally assigned at age 16 and will be required when you start work. It will appear on your payslip, P60 form and letters from HMRC.

Pay As You Earn (PAYE)
If you work for an employer, income tax and National Insurance are automatically deducted from your monthly earnings via the PAYE system.

Tax code
Your tax code tells your employer how much tax to deduct from your pay. It also reflects how much tax-free income (Personal Allowance) you get in that tax year.

PAYE coding notice
A notice from HMRC stating your tax code and how it was worked out.

P45
A form you get from your employer when you stop working for them. It shows how much tax you have paid on your salary so far in that tax year. Keep hold of it, because you'll need to give a copy of your P45 to your next employer.

P60
An annual summary from your employer, showing your salary, tax payments and any other deductions e.g. student loan repayments

Self Assessment
A tax collection system for the self-employed, or when tax cannot be collected through PAYE (e.g. if you owe tax on savings, investments or income from abroad). The taxpayer files a tax return once a year and pays income tax and National Insurance directly to HMRC.

Unique Taxpayer Reference (UTR)
A 10 digit number that HMRC uses to identify you or your company. You only have a UTR if you submit a Self Assessment tax return e.g. because you're self-employed.

Personal Tax Account
Whether you're an employee or self-employed, you can set up an account to manage your tax affairs and interact with HMRC online.

How do freelancers pay taxes?

If you're self-employed, which includes freelancers and contractors, you won't get a pay slip, and the administration and responsibility for paying tax is down to you. It's your responsibility to complete and file a tax return on time to HMRC and then to pay what you owe by the required deadlines. Note that you may be able to claim reliefs and allowances (there's plenty of information about that on hmrc/gov.uk). Lots of self-employed people pay a qualified accountant to help them complete and submit their tax returns to minimise the risk of mistakes and to make sure they're not overpaying.

Useful & unbiased resources for financial information & help

MoneyHelper
A free service, set up by the Government. Whilst they can't give specific product recommendations, they do offer unbiased advice on financial matters including some guides tailored to graduates e.g. managing your money, repaying your student loan, graduate bank accounts. moneyhelper.org.uk

MoneySavingExpert
Founded by journalist and presenter Martin Lewis. A good comparison website, which includes a deals and vouchers section, money-saving guides, tips and tools. moneysavingexpert.com

Citizens Advice
Free confidential advice online, over the phone, and in person on financial matters such as debt, benefits and tax. citizensadvice.org.uk

GOV.UK
Comprehensive information and guidance from Government departments and services, including money and tax, benefits, pensions, business and self-employment. gov.uk

Which? Money
Free online advice plus reviews of financial products and services. There's also a Money Helpline for independent one-to-one guidance on all sorts of money matters over the phone. which.co.uk/money

The information in this book does not constitute any form of advice or recommendation. Always do your research and seek independent, professional advice for your particular situation from a qualified professional or organisation.

10

FLYING THE NEST

...again

For many grads, moving out of the family home is the next big life goal after graduating and finding a job. If you've lived away from home at uni and tasted freedom, you'll be all the more geared up to save up and fly the nest once more!

Although you've probably had a taste of the rental market already, there are some key differences between renting at uni and non-student rentals. In this chapter we'll take you through all that and more, covering how to find a place and like-minded people to live with, what your rights and responsibilities are, the costs and how to avoid the pitfalls, too.

THE RENTING PROCESS:
what to expect...

Prepare to search
Create your brief: decide your budget and search criteria

Start looking
Search free apps and websites, contact letting agents and ask around

View & assess properties
Does it fit your brief, can you afford it, what's the neighbourhood like? Take care to avoid rental scams!

Make an offer
In writing, outline rental amount and key details of the tenancy plus any requests e.g. furniture repairs and professional clean.

Let agreed (subject to contract)

Pay holding deposit to reserve the property if requested. Tenant references are checked and contract is finalised.

Sign the tenancy agreement

Landlord and tenants sign the contract. Pay your security deposit and first month's rent

Prepare to move in

Contact utilities and service providers in advance. On moving day, agree check-in inventory. Read meters and give energy provider your readings.

Enjoy your new home!

FIRST STEPS:

Time to get organised

Although house hunting is the fun part, don't skip the getting organised bit. Most rented homes move fast and, if you find something you like, you could be living in it within three or four weeks, so hold off until you've worked out your budget and decided what sort of place best suits your needs and lifestyle. Following these steps should help...

1. ESTABLISH YOUR PRIORITIES

Choosing the right place encompasses many factors: affordability, who you're going to live with, what type of accommodation you want, comfort, safety, neighbourhood, local amenities, social life and nights out, proximity to the places you go the most, commute time and transport options, parking... there's a lot to consider!

You need to decide what's most important to you, so you can make a list of essential criteria for your property search (e.g. number of bedrooms and bathrooms, whether or not you need outdoor space). If you're flathunting with friends, you should also decide what factors you're willing to compromise on, and what are non-negotiable. Writing a clear brief means you're less likely to waste time traipsing around unsuitable properties.

2. WORK OUT YOUR BUDGET & ORGANISE YOUR FINANCES

You'll need to budget more than just the rent: there are on-going living costs and the initial outlay of taking on a tenancy to consider. You'll need to pay a deposit upfront (you should get this back when you leave; more on that later!), as well as the first month's rent in advance. Then you'll need to factor in the cost of furniture and any equipment – such as a bed, desk, TV, chair, curtains, kitchen paraphernalia – that you might not already own.

love this place

First home!

3. KNOW WHERE TO SEARCH

There are dozens of well-established property websites and apps that let you search for rooms in flat and house shares as well as whole properties, including SpareRoom, Ideal Flatmate, Zoopla and Rightmove, as well as classified ad sites like Gumtree. Set your criteria so that you receive alerts as soon as new ads go live, especially if you're hunting in areas where demand is high and properties go quickly. You can also sign up with local letting agents and give them your brief.

TIP:

Widen your search as much as possible. You might have your heart set on living in one desirable part of a city, but if you look at properties a mere 15-minute walk away, slightly lengthening your commute, the rent might drop considerably.

4. UNDERSTAND THE DIFFERENT OPTIONS

Joint vs sole tenants

Most people rent as tenants, paying a landlord each month, though the property itself may be managed by a letting agent.

Sole tenants rent a room from a landlord, while **joint tenants rent the whole house, together.**

There are pros and cons to both. **As joint tenants, the whole household is responsible for sticking to the terms of the contract.** That means if one person doesn't pay rent, you're all responsible. And if one of you wants to move out, you'll need to notify the landlord, find a new flatmate, and sign a new contract. That's why you really need to know and trust the people you enter into a joint agreement with.

Sole tenants aren't responsible for the other housemates so it can be a simpler arrangement than a joint tenancy. But it's also up to the landlord

to fill empty rooms when someone leaves, meaning you're less likely to get a say in who your housemates are.

Joint and sole tenants will get what's called an **Assured Shorthold Tenancy (AST)** which is the most common type of agreement and offers better protection than other living arrangements.

Lodging

Another option is to **rent a room in a property with a live-in landlord**, as a lodger. You'll have **fewer rights** – including a shorter notice period to leave the property – and house rules are up to the homeowner: there may be restrictions around having guests over, or using shared facilities. **But lodging can be cheaper** and, with the right landlord, it can be a win-win set up.

Guardianship

In recent years, property guardianship has become more popular as people look for ways to live more cheaply, but it's not for everyone. All sorts of **empty properties are available for affordable rent**; in return you provide a service simply by living there, to **look after the property** and deter squatters and vandals. They include residential homes, whose owners are living abroad, and commercial buildings like schools and offices which are awaiting redevelopment.

You might live cheaply in some sizeable spaces, but there are drawbacks: if the building was not designed for residential accommodation, facilities and hygiene might not be up to scratch; there may be rules around leaving the property unoccupied and a short notice period to vacate. **Plus, you're basically live-in security, so it's not for the faint hearted**.

With any renting arrangement, do your research and read and understand the small print of any paperwork. If unclear, get advice and never sign anything you don't understand. See p.206 for where to find help.

FINDING YOUR NEW PAD
Let the viewings begin!

You've got your brief, you've signed up for alerts, and you're raring to go. Let the viewings commence! The most important things to think about when assessing the suitability of a place are:

Affordability

Would renting here fall within my budget?

Location

Does the area feel safe and is it convenient for my lifestyle?

Property

Is it in good condition and does it fit my brief?

Landlord/Agent

Can I confirm they are who they say they are?

SAFETY FIRST.

Particularly if you're meeting a landlord, rather than dealing with a reputable lettings agent, never view a property on your own if you can help it: always take a friend. If you have no choice but to go alone, make sure you give someone the full details of the place and person you're meeting, and make an arrangement to call them after the viewing.

Affordability

We've already mentioned rent, deposit and fees. On top of that you'll need to budget for bills. Occasionally the landlord covers some bills and these are included in the rent but in many cases, especially joint tenancies, you'll have to sort out the bills between you.

And, remember, it may be possible to negotiate on the rent advertised. It doesn't always work, but it's definitely worth asking. It can help if you know the going rates for the area, so do some research before the viewing.

"When I first started renting, I didn't know the process, I wasn't aware that you could put forward an offer, that you can negotiate on the price they're asking. Why would you know if you've never done it before?"

Lotty,
Lettings
Agent

What does renting cost?

Tenancy costs

✳ **A refundable holding deposit** (usually equivalent to one week's rent*)
You might be asked to pay a holding deposit to reserve a property while the contract is prepared. Before you pay or sign anything, make sure you understand the terms e.g. will you get your money back if you change your mind about moving in? Rules on the amount of holding deposit and refunds vary around the UK, so check what applies in your area.

✳ **A security deposit** (usually equivalent to four or five weeks' rent in England*)

*Some agents or landlords might suggest a **zero deposit option**, also known as deposit replacement insurance. Instead of a big deposit, you'll pay a smaller fee (normally equivalent to one week's rent) to cover the cost of the insurance policy. Sounds great in theory, but you may end up paying more in the long run because, unlike a deposit, this fee is non refundable. And, at the end of the tenancy, you may be chased by the insurance company for money the landlord has claimed, for things like damage or cleaning the property you've just left. Similarly, some offer an **option for paying your deposit monthly** instead of upfront but, once again, this option could cost more overall, because you don't get your money back at the end of the tenancy. If you're struggling to save a deposit, look at your local council's website; some have rent deposit schemes that can help.*

✳ **Tenant fees*** Your landlord or agent may be entitled to charge certain fees, which must be stated in your contract e.g. for replacing lost keys or late rent payments

*Caps on deposits and what tenant fees are permitted vary between England, Scotland, Wales and Northern Ireland, so do check the rules for where you're renting. If you think you have been charged unfairly, contact your local Citizens Advice or Shelter.

Ongoing living costs

✳ **Rent** (usually paid one month in advance)

✳ **Council Tax**
You may be unfamiliar with council tax, as students don't have to pay it, but it helps fund local services such as rubbish collection, street lighting, police and fire brigade. The amount you pay is set by your local council and depends on the tax band your property falls into (based on its value). Ask your landlord or agent which council tax band applies or check online by postcode. You could be entitled to a discount or exemptions if you live on your own, claim benefits or earn a low income, or if any of your housemates are full-time students.

✳ **Utility bills**
Energy (electricity and gas), phone, broadband and TV packages, water. Use comparison websites to switch suppliers and get the best possible deals. For water, there's only one supplier and it'll either be metered or a flat rate.

✳ **TV licence**

✳ **Parking permit** (in some cases)

✳ **Insurance**
You'll need home contents cover; there are insurance policies created especially for renters.

Location

Some of this may seem obvious, but it's worth checking that the surrounding area suits your needs. Start with transport links. How long would your commute take? Is there free car parking allocated, or do you have to pay for a permit? How much would it cost?

Check out the local amenities. Is there a shop nearby for emergency food/wine/snack runs, a decent pub, a park, any sports facilities?

Walk around the neighbourhood. If you can, speak to some people who live there. What is it like? How safe does the area feel? Would you be confident walking alone after dark?

What can you see nearby? Are there any potential hazards or nuisance factors e.g. bad smells, pollution, building work, railway lines?

Good green space nearby

35 mins on bus to work

Nearest supermarket: 7 min walk

Nearest pub: 5 min walk

Cool area!

Only one entrance

Property

When you're inside the property use your senses! **What can you hear?** Listen for neighbours through the walls, traffic noise, barking dogs or anything else. **What can you see?** Any signs of water damage, mould on the carpets? **What can you smell?** That unmistakable odour of damp, stale cigarette smoke? Hopefully the answer is 'no' to all of the above!

LOOK OUT FOR DAMP. CHECK UNDER CURTAINS AND FEEL IF THEY'RE COLD OR STICKY, THAT'S USUALLY A SIGN. SO IS PAINT FLAKING AWAY FROM THE WALL; AND YOU CAN SMELL IT IN THE AIR TOO.

– BRONWEN, DESIGNER

“ It's worth really scrutinising the place. I'm a bit of an impulse buyer and thought the house was perfect, but my boyfriend noticed mildew and a loose pipe.

Also, find out about council tax: sometimes it's astronomical! Notice how warm the place is, whether there's insulation or double glazing, because that'll make a huge difference to your bills. ”

Louise,
Business Development Manager

One of the top things to be aware of is security. Are there good locks on the front door and ground floor windows? Is there a burglar alarm? Are the windows double glazed? What is next to the building? If it's public land, an alley or a footpath, how well protected is the property? You can check the crime rate for specific postcodes online.

There's a lot to take in at viewings, so it's a good idea to go prepared with a list of important points to check and questions to ask, so you don't forget anything. We recommend the ones on the next page...

VIEWINGS CHECKLIST

Questions to ask & things to check at property viewings

Tenancy

- [ ] Availability
- [ ] How long has property been on the market? If it's been vacant for ages, why?
- [ ] Length of tenancy
- [ ] Renewable?
- [ ] Break clause – if you need
- [ ] Notice period for ending tenancy
- [ ] Any special clauses in the tenancy agreement to be aware of? E.g. no smoking, no pets?

Landlord/Letting Agent

- [ ] Who is the landlord & where are they based?
- [ ] Who manages the property? Accessibility, emergency contact
- [ ] Registration – professional body/ accreditation scheme
- [ ] Prior experience of letting & managing property?
- [ ] Manner – note whether they are helpful & answer your questions

Costs

Rent

- [ ] How much?
- [ ] Any bills included?
- [ ] Additional costs?
- [ ] How much rent in advance?

Security Deposit *

- [ ] How much?
- [ ] Where will deposit be protected?

Fees & Charges *

- [ ] Do you charge any other fees? E.g. replacing lost keys
- [ ] Holding deposit? Under what circumstances is it refundable?

*Check that deposits & fees comply with regulations (varies for different parts of the UK)

Bills

- [ ] Council tax – which band applies?
- [ ] Utilities: Energy Efficiency Rating – ask to see EPC (Energy Performance Certificate)

Insurance

- [ ] What cover does landlord have (buildings)?
- [ ] What cover do tenants need (contents)?

The Area

- [ ] Transport, commute
- [ ] Amenities, shops, leisure
- [ ] What's nearby? Any potential problems e.g. pollution, flooding, noise, traffic, railway, commercial buildings?
- [ ] Safety – would you feel safe coming home late? Check crime rate
- [ ] Neighbours – elderly, children?

The Property

General Condition

Check if the property seems to be well-maintained:

- [ ] Outside e.g. check for missing roof tiles, leaking pipes & gutters, flaking paintwork
- [ ] Inside e.g. any visible signs or smell of damp? Check for draughts, loose wires, flaking paintwork, shabby décor, hygiene & cleanliness

Features & Facilities

- [ ] Bedrooms – number & size
- [ ] Facilities – living area, kitchen, bathrooms
- [ ] Furnishings & curtains – what's included?

Fixtures & fittings

- [ ] What's included? White goods e.g. washer, dryer, fridge, microwave.
- [ ] What is the heating system?
- [ ] Check the water pressure in the shower & taps
- [ ] Are there enough power points?
- [ ] Is there a telephone landline?

Outside

- [ ] Parking
- [ ] Communal areas (flats) – whose responsibility? Service charges?
- [ ] Garden – whose responsibility?

Safety

- [ ] Gas safety certificate – when was the last gas safety check carried out & can I see the certificate? (By law this must be done every 12 months)
- [ ] Electricity & gas meters – where are they located?
- [ ] Electrics PAT (Portable Appliance Testing certificates)
- [ ] Fire safety – smoke alarms, carbon monoxide alarms, chimneys
- [ ] Boiler – when last serviced?
- [ ] Where is the water stopcock?
- [ ] Security – is there an alarm?
- [ ] What sort of locks on the windows & doors?
- [ ] Check windows open & close & aren't painted shut
- [ ] Adjoining area – what borders the property? How safe?
- [ ] Any previous problems e.g. burglaries, flooding?

If you do notice any necessary repairs, problems or potential issues, ask for them to be addressed before you move in, and have this written into your contract.

Landlord/Agent

Some rentals are managed by letting agencies whilst others involve you dealing directly with a private landlord. **Before you sign a contract or pay anything, you need to be sure that the person you're dealing with is genuine and legally entitled to let the property.** You also want the person handling your tenancy to be fair, helpful and accessible.

Ideally, you'd rent through a **reputable** letting agent or a landlord who has been **recommended** to you. But that's not always possible. Instead, you can read **online reviews** of agents and **speak to the current tenants** if you get the chance. Look for landlords and letting agents who are signed up to a **professional body or accreditation scheme**, which shows they take their responsibilities seriously. Plus,

members of these schemes must adhere to a code of conduct. Do check with the relevant organisation to verify their membership.

You can also check the landlord really is the homeowner through the **Land Registry**. You may ask for the landlord's name and UK contact address even if the property is being managed by an agent.

Always **exercise caution**, particularly if you decide to rent directly through a landlord. In the current climate where demand far exceeds supply, scammers hope people will cut corners and pay up immediately to secure a property. Don't be tempted!

BEWARE RENT SCAMMERS

Posing as landlords, some scammers arrange viewings (having broken in or rented the property themselves). They will often ask for money upfront, tricking multiple prospective tenants into handing over deposits and advance rent payments, before disappearing without trace. Fortunately scams are relatively rare, but scammers do still manage to get listings on reputable websites and apps, so it's worth knowing the telltale signs.

> Does the rent seem too good to be true? Then it probably is. It's worth knowing the going rate for the area, as this will help you spot dodgy ads a mile off!

> Beware if the listing or their written communications are full of typos or poor grammar, or if they avoid answering your questions. Genuine landlords or agents will take care to communicate properly.

> Are they hassling you for a deposit, holding fee or the first month's rent before even meeting you? A good landlord will want to meet you to make sure you're a decent person who will look after their property (just as you will want to know that they seem friendly and helpful). They will also have a screening process, normally asking you for references and a credit check. If they don't, this should ring alarm bells!

> Many scammers will request money by wire transfer services like Western Union and MoneyGram, which is a bit like sending cash because the recipient and the transactions are very hard to trace and cannot be reversed. Reputable landlords and agents will typically ask for money to be sent by bank transfer, although some agents do accept debit and credit cards.

> And never send money overseas in return for a promise that the keys will be sent to you. That's highly likely to be a scam!

> Don't be put off by excuses that you can't view a property, however plausible they seem e.g. redecorating, no one available to show you round, inconvenient for the current tenants. You should always view a property, at least twice, before signing anything. If you're unable to go yourself, get someone you trust to see it. An increasing number of agents and property websites are offering virtual reality viewings, but it's never a substitute for thoroughly checking out the property and surrounding area, to make sure you would be happy living there and to ensure it's not a scam.

" Never ever commit to a property without having seen it. Get an idea of who the landlord is as well, that's important. Are they going to be able to come and fix stuff or get someone in when things break down? Some landlords prefer to have the rental professionally managed by an agent. If you've got an international landlord who doesn't have the property managed, that's not the best scenario. **"**

Lotty,
Lettings Agent

NEVER PAY ANY MONEY OR SIGN AN AGREEMENT UNTIL:

✓ You have viewed the property (twice at least)

✓ You are certain that the landlord/letting agent is genuine

✓ You have agreed the rent and other costs

✓ You understand and agree with all the terms and conditions of the contract

How To Find Housemates

One of the best things about renting is the **social aspect**. Loads of renters move in with people they've never met before, have a brilliant time and make friends for life. **Choose who you live with carefully, as you'll be spending a lot of time with them!**

There are plenty of flat and house share sites that'll buddy you up with housemates, including SpareRoom and Ideal Flatmate.. **Take the time to chat to people you match with** on the phone, meet up for a coffee and make sure the conversation flows.

For a harmonious household you'll need to find people who have similar expectations and lifestyles. Think about how you live and ask potential housemates the same questions about themselves. For example, are you OCD about cleaning or do you not mind a bit of mess? Do you think paying for a cleaner is a good investment? Do you want to cook meals and go to the pub with your housemates? Are you a strict vegan who would find living with carnivorous housemates unthinkable? It's also worth asking what hours your potential housemates typically work. If you want to live in a sociable house and you work 9-5, it's no good moving in with people who work nights.

Sometimes, you'll view a room in an existing joint tenancy that someone has just left. Meeting a bunch of housemates with a spare room can be fun if you get on. Or, it can feel like an interview, a personality test and a bun fight combined! **Just be yourself and if you don't get the room, it wasn't meant to be.**

Just remember, only sign up for a joint tenancy **with people you really trust**, because all of you are jointly legally responsible for the property. If someone fails to pay, you could be pursued for their share!

When you finally see a ray of light, some decent humans/housemates in a seemingly lovely house and at a steal of a price, take a moment to process. Make sure you do actually still check that everything about the place is right and ask all the appropriate questions about bills etc. I got so over excited that I'd finally found a normal place with like-minded people, that I failed to notice the inch-thick dust on all the carpets thanks to the lack of a hoover in the house during the six months they'd lived there (grim!). Oozing shower mould, cigarette smoke-filled curtains and, well, you get my drift.

Georgina,
Account Director

Living with friends means you don't feel as lonely: you feel like you've got some support. We do have a cooking rota, so we share meals which adds to the team spirit. Some are better cooks than others, but nothing has been that inedible so far!

Adam, Investment Manager

YOUR TENANCY EXPLAINED

The landlord and tenants should all sign a proper tenancy agreement which sets out the **terms and conditions** i.e. the length, the rent payment terms, the security deposit and your rights and responsibilities.

Before signing, read it through carefully to make sure that you've understood and that you agree with everything on it. If anything is unclear, don't be afraid to ask questions. If you have any doubts or concerns, consult someone you trust who is knowledgeable about renting, or Citizens Advice. The charity Shelter also has some great resources on its website and check GOV.UK for more info about renting law.

Most tenancies are a 'fixed term' and 12 months is standard, though you could request longer. If you want a shorter tenancy, you can ask for a break clause which usually allows either you or the landlord to give notice to end the tenancy early. This can be useful if your career plan is uncertain and you don't want to be tied in for a whole year.

Security Deposit

You will be asked to pay a security deposit before moving in, to give your landlord some protection in case you damage the property or leave without paying the rent. It's normally four to five weeks' rent in England but it varies in other parts of the UK, so check the rules for where you're searching.

As long as you keep to the terms of the tenancy agreement, your deposit must be refunded in full. Your landlord is not allowed to keep your deposit in their bank account. Instead, they have to put it in a **tenancy deposit scheme**, which keeps your money safe, and ensures tenants are treated fairly if there is any dispute over returning the deposit at the end of the tenancy. Your landlord must confirm where your deposit is being held.

Inventory

When you move into your new home, you should receive a detailed inventory, which is just a **record of everything in the property** – like furniture, fixtures and fittings – and what condition they're in. You'll need to check this over, make sure you agree with everything and, if you don't, suggest changes. Keep records, take photos and, if no inventory is provided, write it yourself, email it to the landlord or agent and ask them to sign it off, as it's **really important for avoiding disputes**. At the end of your tenancy, you'll need to leave the property in the same condition to get your whole deposit back.

TOP TIP:
Keep copies of all documents, emails and any correspondence with landlords and agents. If you discuss anything over the phone, summarise the conversation in an email and ask them to acknowledge the contents. That way, if there is ever a dispute, you'll have a paper trail to show.

Read your tenancy agreement carefully!

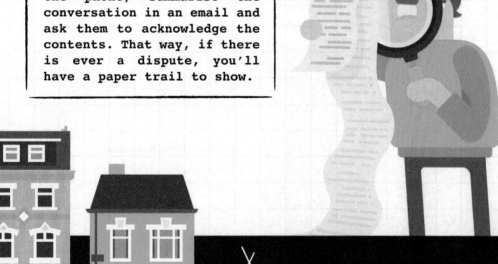

Where to find help

If you have any problems, there are plenty of places you can turn for professional help and expert guidance.

Issues with your landlord/agent

For more information on your rights and handling issues with your landlord, try Citizens Advice. Resources available at **citizensadvice.org.uk/housing**, plus online chat and a phone line.

An independent ombudsman service can help resolve disputes between the tenants and the landlord or letting agent, without needing to go to court. Private landlords should have a complaints procedure, but if this fails to achieve an acceptable outcome, the Housing Ombudsman Service (HOS) can help with problems concerning its members. **housing-ombudsman.org.uk**

Frauds & Scams

If you have been conned out of money, or threatened, contact Action Fraud, the UK's national fraud and crime reporting centre | **0300 123 20 40**

General help & advice

For expert housing advice, chat to the charity Shelter online | **Shelter.org.uk**

PREPARING TO MOVE:

Who to inform

From removals companies to your bank, electoral roll, student loans, and your employer, there are plenty of companies and suppliers you'll need to contact with your change of address. This doesn't take long, but it's easy to forget a few so we've created the moving checklist at the end of this chapter to help you work out what needs sorting. Some services require a few days or even weeks to activate, so it's better to let them know your requirements before you move in.

HAPPY NEW HOME!

MOVING CHECKLIST

Things to sort & people to contact

Landlord/Letting Agency

- [ ] Contact details
- [ ] Tenancy agreement
- [ ] Deposit certificate
- [ ] Inventory
- [ ] Energy Performance Certificate (EPC)
- [ ] Gas Safety Certificate

Rent

- [ ] Standing order

Local Authority

- [ ] Council tax – address & payment method
- [ ] Electoral roll

Utilities

Gas

- [ ] Meter reading
- [ ] Address & payment method

Electricity

- [ ] Meter reading
- [ ] Address & payment method

Water

- [ ] Meter reading (if applicable)
- [ ] Address & payment method

Telephone & Broadband

- [ ] Landline – address, number transfer & payment method
- [ ] Broadband/internet – address & payment method
- [ ] Mobile – address & payment method

TV

- [ ] Licence
- [ ] Cable / satellite / digital provider – address & payment method

Insurance

- [ ] Contents
- [ ] Buildings – landlord's responsibility (check)

Motoring

- [ ] Parking permit
- [ ] DVLA – driving licence
- [ ] Insurance
- [ ] Breakdown Cover

Health

- [ ] Doctor
- [ ] Dentist

Finance

- [ ] Bank
- [ ] Credit
- [ ] HMRC – tax & National Insurance
- [ ] Student Loan Company
- [ ] Pension

Employer

- [ ] HR / payroll

Postal Service

- [ ] Mail redirection

Removals

- [ ] Book a service?
- [ ] Check insurance cover

Other

- [ ]
- [ ]

11

FINAL
Thoughts

What is success?

We put a lot of pressure on ourselves to be 'successful', but what does success really look like?

Success is entirely subjective, there's no 'one size fits all' definition: some people may be motivated by money and acquiring things like a big house and fast car; others would like to achieve recognition or fame, or power and status. For some people, it's about making a difference, helping others and giving back; and some of us want to hone a particular skill, craft, instrument or sport until we are the best we can possibly be.

For this book, we spoke to hundreds of people from recent graduates to experienced professionals, to ask what success means to them, and whether their views have changed over time, to help us understand why we do what we do.

And almost everyone has come to the same conclusion...

All of them said that, early on when they'd just left education, they saw success as something fairly specific (and often material): getting a job with a top company, playing sport to a professional level, being paid a big bonus, achieving early promotion, or earning more than their friends.

But as they gained some life experience, or overcame challenges, their measures of success changed into this simple realisation: that **success is being truly happy in what you're doing and how you're living your life.**

Success may be defined by your career. Or it might be something else entirely. Some people find joy and their sense of purpose through work, while others do a job that is an enabler, allowing them to earn enough money to find fulfilment elsewhere, pursuing a passion or interest that has nothing to do with their day job. Both paths are great.

If you try to make decisions based on what makes you happy, rather than someone else's arbitrary measure of success, or your own preconceived ideas of what success should look like, you'll soon have a healthy sense of direction fuelling you.

* do more of what you love *

I used to think success meant earning the highest wage, being in a high-profile job and generally winning at all aspects of life. When you leave uni, you realise that really, nobody is living a perfect image of 'success' (and if it looks like they are on social media, then trust me, it's not showing the full picture). I think success is all about finding contentment. It isn't overwhelming happiness (because who feels that all the time?) it's actually just tuning into the present moment and realising that you're doing just fine where you are, you're proud of how far you've come, and you're looking forward to the future.

"For some, that contentment might be a fast-paced job where you earn a lot and progress rapidly. But for others, it could mean a job you really enjoy, that doesn't make you stressed or lose out on precious time with friends and family. Success looks entirely different for everyone, and for me, it's just knowing that I have the resources to be happy where I am in the present moment.

Sophie, Graduate Policy Adviser

On tour with the boys

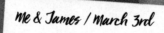

Me & James / March 3rd

Rebecca's 22nd B-day

life is about the journey

Drinks in the sun!

Family beach trip!

Spring has sprung

The money shot!

Night out / May 12th

That longggg walk

You've got this...

Many of us will admit to obsessing over the endgame, or future gazing when we should be grounding ourselves in the present and **enjoying the here and now.**

Living through troubled times has highlighted that we don't always know what lies ahead, and that many things are outside our control. It's given most of us a fresh sense of perspective, teaching us to find happiness in what we have, and with whatever we're doing at the present moment, rather than thinking we need to rush to change everything.

Rather than viewing life as a series of stepping stones to something better, or enduring circumstances for a bigger payoff later, we can instead focus on the process – because that's the most meaningful part. **Life is about the journey**, not the destination. While having goals is crucial for giving us direction, we must also enjoy the ride and make the time to reflect as we go along.

Your career may be dominating your thoughts at the moment, but it is only one part of the picture. More important is discovering what you love and working out how to do more of it, and reaching a healthy work-life balance (it's non-negotiable for good mental health). So too is making time for your friends and family. They'll support you when times are tough and share and revel in the many joys of life.

Be open to opportunities, they can take you in a direction that you might not have considered. Equally, don't be afraid to make changes if you're unhappy where you are. What is most important is to do what feels best for you at the time and to learn and grow from each experience.

Right here, right now is where you're meant to be. Whatever you choose to do next, remember you're on a long journey, one that's unique to you, which may look nothing like the paths your friends and fellow grads are on. **Be proud of how far you've come**, and be hopeful for the future. You have every reason to be.

right here, right now is where you're meant to be

"When I left uni it was all about finding that perfect job, finding your passion and doing it forever. That's what I thought success was. But it's really changed now, partly because I've realised that people have more than one passion. Some people, like artists, are lucky because they can do what drives them, throughout their life. But for me, having one passion is not how I work, it's not who I am, I like a lot of things. Success for me is a feeling of harmony and acceptance for whatever you're doing at the present moment.

"You can spend all your time thinking my life isn't quite good enough, I need to change things, the future is always going to be better. But even if it's not perfect, having that acceptance, making room for happiness, rather than feeling you've got to change everything - that's what success means for me."

Chloë, Early Careers Coach

"Success is finding something that makes you whistle on the way to work, rather than whistle as you are leaving."

Jill, Headteacher

SUCCESS IS BEING TRULY HAPPY IN WHAT YOU'RE DOING AND HOW YOU'RE LIVING YOUR LIFE

"It's good to have money and the things that money can buy, but it's good, too, to check up once in a while and make sure that you haven't lost the things that money can't buy."

George Lorimer, Journalist & Author

"Success is the ability to do what you love every day. This may sound simple but what you love changes over time and having the ability to change what you are doing to match your passion is true success. This has nothing to do with money, wealth or status as each person has different passions and loves."

David Hauser, Co-Founder of Grasshopper
(Source: under30ceo.com)

"Back in the day, I would have seen money as a yardstick of success. If I got a pay rise, that would mean I am successful. If my friend was earning more than me, I would consider him more successful. As I've got older, it's more about doing something that really interests you. Setting yourself a challenge and succeeding in that is a greater success than a large bonus. I would say it has moved from quantifiable money to experience and learning."

Michael, Innovation Consultant

"SUCCESS EQUALS HAPPINESS. BUT IT USED TO BE ABOUT WINNING EVERYTHING. ASK BUSINESS PEOPLE WHEN LAST THEY GOT EXCITED IN THE BUSINESS WORLD, THEY POSSIBLY COULDN'T TELL YOU. I HAVE A JOB AND LIFESTYLE THAT EXCITES ME EVERY DAY. WHEN THAT STOPS, I'LL STOP."

MATT, FORMER HOCKEY INTERNATIONAL TURNED COACHING BUSINESS OWNER

"Before, the way I measured success was quantifiable: my next pay rise, a promotion, how well I did in my personal development plan. But now it's smaller things that make me happy: daily interactions with people in my community, landing a job I love even if it means a week of low pay, teaching a great yoga session, receiving amazing feedback after a class – that gives me so much more gratification and happiness than a 1% pay rise. Now it's the smaller things in life that keep me motivated, and that's how I measure success, rather than career progression or big business ideas."

Hannah, Yoga Teacher, Designer
& Business Founder

" Happiness is not in the mere possession of money ; it lies in the joy of achievement, in the thrill of creative effort."

Franklin D. Roosevelt
Former US President

"IT SOUNDS LIKE A CLICHÉ, BUT I THINK SUCCESS IS FEELING HAPPY AND FULFILLED WITHIN YOUR LIFE. MY VIEW ON SUCCESS HAS DEFINITELY CHANGED OVER TIME, PARTICULARLY DURING THE PANDEMIC WHICH THREW INTO PERSPECTIVE WHAT'S REALLY IMPORTANT.

"TRY NOT TO COMPARE YOUR LIFE AND ACHIEVEMENTS TO OTHERS, AS COMPARISON TRULY IS THE THIEF OF JOY. EVERYONE IS ON THEIR OWN PATH AND SUCCESS EBBS AND FLOWS, SO YOU'VE JUST GOT TO STAY FOCUSED, WORK HARD BUT ALSO HAVE FUN AND NOT BE TOO TOUGH ON YOURSELF."

VICTORIA, SOCIAL MEDIA MARKETING BUSINESS OWNER

"What you shouldn't do is worry about what everyone else thinks. You'll have individual goals and if you can achieve those goals, then that is success. It could be work-related, perhaps getting more responsibility, becoming a team leader; or personal objectives like running a half-marathon. It may be the smallest goal or the biggest – any win is a win!

"I'd say don't put too much pressure on yourself. A lot of people feel under pressure to find a job, get a place and start living. Really don't worry. Take your time. Rejection will happen but success will follow."

Doug, Financial Trader

"IT DOESN'T MATTER ABOUT MONEY; HAVING IT, NOT HAVING IT. OR HAVING CLOTHES, OR NOT HAVING THEM. YOU'RE STILL LEFT ALONE WITH YOURSELF IN THE END."

BILLY IDOL, MUSICIAN

"A career is your lifetime of work. You could have one job, or you could have many. Our circumstances change as we go through life — different influences, loved ones, family situation, priorities. And our careers reflect the changes we experience. People are retraining in their fifties and sixties, so don't be afraid to start anew. The possibilities are endless, there will be jobs that don't exist right now. Maybe you'll have a passion you can develop into a career, or a business.

"Just don't get hung up if you're not where you once hoped to be and don't just measure yourself by others' achievements. A successful career is one you're happy doing."

Mark, Career Coach

ACKNOWLEDGMENTS

Producing a book was harder than we thought, but it was also immensely enjoyable and rewarding. Researching and writing kept us sane (relatively!) through lockdowns and beyond. We would like to thank everyone who helped us.

Firstly, we'd like to express our deepest gratitude to our fellow creators of this book – you're the best!

Emily Garnham, for your eloquent writing, meticulous editing and constant inspiration, and for being an all-round great person to have on the team, who helped make this a really fun ride. We couldn't have done it without you, and we hope you know just how much we appreciate your contribution to this book.

Lizzy Tasker, our talented designer. You totally 'got it' and it has been a delight working with you. We were always excited to receive the next completed chapter design. And we were never disappointed. Your work has brought the book to life, thank you so much Lizzy.

Chris Gilleard, whose illustrations light up the pages, adding a touch of humour to heavier topics and making us laugh at ourselves. You're such a talent, thank you for giving our book its personality, which words alone could never do.

We are always extremely thankful for our wonderful family: Peter, Adam, Elena and Michael (and Deia), Tom and Jess, Jill, Renie, Katie, Simon and Gabriel (and never forgetting Peter and Norman RIP). For your never-ending love, support and encouragement; and on a practical level for being our guineapigs, proof-readers, honest critics and fervent cheerleaders - huge thanks and love to you all.

A special mention to some other great people who have collaborated with us on the HelloGrads student/graduate platform, which motivated us to write the book:

Ross Tuffee, for helping us get things off the ground, your belief in the project, your inspiration, encouragement, and infectious enthusiasm for life in general. Colin Mackenzie, tech genius, you are also an excellent communicator, demystifying coding and other incomprehensible gobbledygook for us supremely untechy humans!

Charli May, we love your can-do attitude and thoroughly appreciate your contribution on so many fronts: from videography and editing, to writing, planning and being a pleasure to work with.

Victoria Drysdale, social media guru, we're so glad we found you. Thank you for your creativity, your smart ideas and for running things so smoothly.

Chris Matchan, for your refreshingly original and inspirational outlook, and your infinite words of wisdom, many of which are dotted around the book.

Andy Barton, for regularly giving up your time to sort our SEO and impart valuable business advice.

We would also like to thank our young team who acted as our focus group, challenging us and helping to develop our thoughts, throwing in plenty of bright ideas along the way: Isabella Cipirska, Mónica Ferreira, Alex McCord, Rosalie Minnitt, Chloe Price and Pippa Stacey.

Finally, to all our other contributors and experts, without whom this book would never have happened. We are extremely grateful for your many invaluable insights, relatable stories and practical tips, and for allowing us to include them in this book:

Hannah Aylett – Designer & Founder of Hannah May Studio; Michael Bean – Strategy & Innovation Consultant; Jon Benjamin – British Diplomat at the Foreign, Commonwealth & Development Office; Alessa Berg – Founder and CEO at Top Tier; Louise Bleach – Business Development Manager at Desolenator; Patrick Burge – Mentor & Business Adviser; Charlene Brown – Employment Lawyer & Founding Partner of Howlett Brown; Rikesh (RKZ) Chauhan - Menswear Writer, Photographer, Musician & Ambassador for mental health charity CALM; Abigail Connor – Senior Digital PR & Promotion Executive; Claire Derry – Business Coach;

Milly Edgerley – Writer; Georgina Everitt – Account Director; Lizzie Fane – Founder of Global Graduates; Chloë Garland – Founder of Quarter-Life career & mindset coaching; Ben Gately – Co-founder of Charlie HR software for small businesses; Ali Gillum – Founder of Ali Gillum Tables events company; Tamsin Gordon - Jewellery business Founder; Jill Grinsted – Sales & Marketing Director; Dennis Harhalakis - Founder of Cambridge Money Coaching; Jill Heller – former Headteacher; Henry Lee - Talent Agent; Lotty Lee – Senior Creative Production Manager; Kalkidan Legesse – Founder of Sancho's, ethical clothing & lifestyle business; Matt Legg – Founder of FC Not Alone, the world's first mental health football club & Ambassador for CALM; Rebecca Livesey – Food Product Developer; Doug Love – Financial Trader; Monica Lucas – Business Adviser; Amber Jane McCormick – Mindfulness Teacher; Penny McIvor – Managing Director & Consultant, Fashion; Bruce McKendrick – Leisure company CEO; Sophie Mitchell – Graduate Policy Adviser, Civil Service; Grace O'Leary – Talent Agent; Peter Phillipson – Chairman of several major leisure businesses; Bronwen Rees – Designer; Mark Rice RCDP – Career Coach; Jess Simpson - Dietitian; Matt Taylor – former Hockey International & Founder of coaching business MT13; Adam Valentine -Investment Manager; Fraser Wood – Digital Strategist; Chloe Wright - Product Manager, Performance Marketing; Nicholas Wyman – Author & CEO of Institute for Workplace Skills & Innovation.

ABOUT THE AUTHORS

Behind this book are mother and daughter team Julie and Sophie Phillipson. The pair founded HelloGrads.com, a hub of information for students and graduates, in 2016, when Sophie and friends were beginning to navigate adult life, hampered by a massive information chasm and lack of life skills. Since then, through the website, social media and events, they have helped thousands of young people ease into life after university. They have worked with universities, careers services, employers and student accommodation providers, building a strong awareness of the issues facing students and graduates. Alongside this professional background, their respective personal experiences (Sophie as a recent graduate and now a teacher, Julie as a mother of three graduates) have given them valuable insights. Over the years, many people suggested they consolidate these into a book and, after the pandemic struck, they felt the time was right. Never have students and graduates needed support more.

For this book, they have also consulted a wide variety of industry experts, from CEOs of multinational companies to entrepreneurs of successful start-ups, recruiters, business advisers, careers services, youth counsellors, banks and letting agents, as well as students, and many graduates who have recently been through the uni-to-work transition themselves. Their input has helped the authors to put together a rich source of information and guidance, to help graduates on their way, and show them that there are many possible routes to success and fulfilment.

Printed in Great Britain
by Amazon

36560914R00123